To

# CRANIUM crisis

## My Compelling Story of Mind Over Matter

*Live,
Laugh,
Love*

**Angela Freriks**

*Angela Freriks*

**CRANIUM CRISIS**
Copyright © 2013 by Angela Freriks

All rights reserved. Neither this publication nor any part of this publication may be reproduced or transmitted in any form or by any means, electronic or mechanical, including photocopying, recording or any information storage and retrieval system, without permission in writing from the author.

Scripture quotations marked (NIV) taken from The Holy Bible, New International Version®, NIV® Copyright © 1973, 1978, 1984, 2011 by Biblica, Inc.™ Used by permission. All rights reserved worldwide. Scripture quotations marked (NKJV) taken from the New King James Version®. Copyright © 1982 by Thomas Nelson, Inc. Used by permission. All rights reserved. Scripture quotations marked (GNB) taken from the Good News Translation® (Today's English Version, Second Edition). Copyright © 1992 American Bible Society. All rights reserved.

Printed in Canada

ISBN: 978-1-77069-719-5

Word Alive Press
131 Cordite Road, Winnipeg, MB R3W 1S1
www.wordalivepress.ca

Library and Archives Canada Cataloguing in Publication

Freriks, Angela, 1972-
    Cranium crisis : a compelling event of mind over matter / Angela Freriks.
ISBN 978-1-77069-719-5

    1. Freriks, Angela, 1972- --Health. 2. Life change events--Psychological aspects. 3. Life change events--Religious aspects--Christianity. 4. Christian biography. I. Title.

BR1725.F74A3 2012        248.8'61092        C2012-904878-X

## Dedication

This book is dedicated to those with brain-related issues and their families. Hats off to all skilled neurosurgeons, surgical teams, and medical students studying neuroscience.

Table of Contents

**introduction** ix

part one 1
part two 55
part three 151

**epilogue** 165
**inspirations and acknowledgements** 169

Even though it has been over twenty years since she passed, my Gramma is still dear to my heart. It seems as though I can hear her audible voice, reading the poem from a bookmark she gave me eons ago:

> When things go wrong, as they sometimes will,
> When the road you're trudging seems all uphill,
> When the funds are low and the debts are high,
> And you want to smile, but you have to sigh,
> When care is pressing you down a bit—
> Rest if you must, but don't you quit.
> Success is failure turned inside out,
> The silver tint of the clouds of doubt,
> And you never can tell how close you are,
> It may be near when it seems afar.
> So, stick to the fight when you're hardest hit—
> It's when things go wrong that you mustn't quit.
> (Author Unknown)

## Introduction

It's a girl! In 1972, I rested for the very first time while being cradled in my mother's arms. As a newborn baby, I was placed in a clear plastic crib. Around my little wrist was a hospital bracelet with the name "Angela" printed on it.

When I was an infant, my parents once entered my bedroom only to find I wasn't in my crib. They looked at each other, astonished, unable to figure out how I had escaped my sleeping quarters. Maybe, subconsciously, I hadn't liked the caged-in feeling. Rather than pose as the Incredible Hulk, trying to pry the bars apart, I had decided to hurl myself over the edge. I don't know what would ever have possessed me to do such a thing. The wooden bars wouldn't hold me captive, even if I had to scale the walls of my crib. My scheming freed me of captivity, so when my parents came in the room I was safely on the floor, content, playing with my toys.

Mom and Dad still reminisce about their strong-willed child. I had a mind of my own, and even if I had to catapult out of my crib, nothing could stand in my way. I don't believe I sustained any head injuries from this particular escape, but after a few crib breaks, my parents figured they should leave the bars down so I didn't hurt myself. With a promise to be out on good behaviour, I never slept behind bars again.

Once I was a toddler, I advanced to a single bed with pictures of Disney characters on my sheets. Should I have happened to roll out of bed, I would have landed on a thick shag carpet with underlay beneath—how bad could that have been?

In the 80s, I jumped into a queen-size waterbed with a deluxe headboard on which I could display my eraser collection. As an adolescent, making the bed never made it onto my priority list. I was a teenager and my bedroom had a feature wall papered with a collage of my favourite boy celebrities.

As a young adult, I moved out of my parents' house. Dad disassembled my waterbed, since I insisted on taking it with me. The waterbed was set up and taken down a few times—that is, until 2007. I had a health scare and ended up in the hospital, downsizing to a single cot with guardrails.

After that, I upgraded to a top-of-the-line Kingsdown with a Euro Top mattress, along with six-hundred-thread-count Egyptian cotton sheets. I wasn't sleeping single, either, as I was now married. Beside my husband, in our plush bed, I was snug as a bug in a rug—until darkness closed in on our perfect ambience. I felt a glitch in my sleep pattern. An unwelcome predator intruded, disrupting my sleep. Not only was it threatening my rest, but it wreaked havoc on my daily life.

I felt like I was drowning in a sea of misery, the waters rising and the waves crashing in a current of chaos. It seemed as though I was caught in the undertow but treading water, fighting to keep my head above water while not letting my symptoms destroy me. I refused help; no one would have to drag the waters. I would not sink in a symphony of suffering.

Whilst on dry land, I hunted for answers to conquer my problem. Life was a chain of challenges: seeking advice from numerous doctors and undergoing medical exams. My feeling of climbing the walls progressed into a decision to face an uphill battle and climb a mountain.

## Cranium Crisis

Eventually, I found myself in an MRI machine, flat on my back. Almost two years later, I was back in my crib (and by that I mean *home*), sinking into our super luxurious king-size bed, recuperating after a long, trying experience. Won't you join me as I narrate my memoirs?

# part one

## Let's Take It from the Top

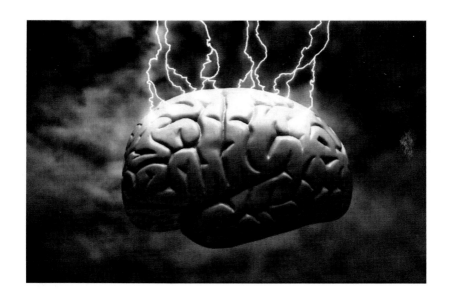

## September 7, 2007

Life was copacetic. I was in the comfort zone of my hometown—Weyburn, Saskatchewan. I owned a house on Brimacombe Drive. The home was equipped with a high-tech alarm system that went by the name Sheena Securities. Sheena, my German shepherd, monitored the place 24/7. I swear she slept with one eye open.

I loved living on the east side of town, where the majority of my clients were only a hop, skip, and a jump away. For my phone number, I purposely selected the last four digits to spell MAID, so no one would forget. "Remember the correct spelling, though; use your noodle," I'd say, pointing my index finger and tapping it on the top of my head.

If I wasn't available, my answering machine would kick in: *"You're in, I'm out. When I get back, I'll give you a shout. You know the drill."* Beeep.

It was a Thursday and I was having a stellar day. I put in a full day's work. I was driving, with the tunes cranked. I rarely got through a whole song before reaching my next destination.

I was at the shop, ready to pull a night shift. I always seemed to be fashionably late for this particular cleaning job. However, when I arrived, there were still a few diehards roaming the premises. One of the guys I'd become good friends with stood by the time clock, ready to punch out. On his blue coveralls was a sewn-on patch which read "Jack." Along with his jumpsuit, he wore a welding beanie.

"Hey, what's up, Beanie Baby?" My voice screeched as I gave him a slap on the back.

Jack was a bit of a prankster, which always made work interesting—and sometimes annoying. I don't know how long he'd been devising this plan, but when I went to the supply room, I couldn't find my mop pail anywhere.

I didn't hesitate to go to the back and ask Jack if he'd seen it. After playing the hot/cold game for several minutes, he was in stitches and couldn't stand it anymore. He just about coughed up a lung while pointing up to the industrial lights. "Obviously, you didn't look *high* and low for your pail!"

I raised my eyes. There was my bright yellow janitor's bucket, hanging way up high. He'd attached the handle to a hook, used the metal chain, and hoisted it up.

I couldn't help but roar. "I wouldn't have found that in a million years!"

He lowered it. When it was steady on the cement floor, I growled, "Careful not to kick the bucket; I'd hate for something unforeseen to happen to you." My threats drifted into thin air as I stooped over, wheeled the pail, and got back to work.

As they say, all work and no play makes Jack a dull boy.

That was the calm before the storm. I had a gut feeling about a weather warning. I could sense dark clouds moving in and possible lightning flashes… I felt weird, kind of dizzy and lightheaded.

I sat down for a minute, figuring I'd been working too hard during the day. I felt like I was going to pass out. If I did, I would have landed on a concrete floor, surrounded by a bunch of parts bins and office supplies. My head spun like I'd just stepped off the swinging chair ride at the fair.

*It's probably nothing,* I told myself. *It'll pass.*

I was almost finished work for the day. Maybe I was just dehydrated or needed to eat something...

*No, this isn't good.*

I wasn't feeling well and felt like I might faint. I cautiously walked around looking for the boss's son. Finding him, I explained that I was done for the day and had to go home. He looked concerned and offered me a ride. I told him I thought I'd be alright to drive. Perhaps I didn't look so well, as he repeated the question, "Are you sure I can't give you a ride?"

"No thanks, I should be okay."

I thought I'd save myself the embarrassment of throwing up in his vehicle.

Stubborn as I was, I got behind the wheel and started home. The drive was only a short distance; I'd be there before I knew it. Usually I took the back way—a gravel road out in the country—but that night I had a feeling I should take the main highway.

"You never get sick," I told myself. "Focus. You're almost home. Thar she blows... there's the city limits."

I had just turned the corner off the highway when I forced myself to pull over. I felt like I was having a panic attack. I put my head on the steering wheel, turned on the hazard lights, and reached for my cell phone. I called my parents' house.

When my dad answered, I blurted, "I'm pulled over on the shoulder of Sixteenth Street. I'm shaking and it feels like my right leg is numb."

"I'm on my way."

Luckily I lived in a small city and was within blocks of both my parents' house and mine. Within minutes, my mom and dad came to my rescue and drove me straight to the hospital.

I made my way up the steps and to the front desk. "Hospitalization card," I heard a voice say. Standing there in a stupor, I never spoke a word. "Do you have your health card with you?"

"No, of course not," I snapped at the receptionist, unhappy to be in this confused state. "I was at work and didn't have my purse with me."

It turned out the lady at the front desk knew me, so she proceeded to punch my name into the computer. My condition wasn't improving, so I leaned against the counter and held my head.

She looked at my parents and asked, "Does she need a wheelchair?" The next thing I knew, they were sitting me down in a chair with really big wheels. I sat in the waiting room with a stupefied look on my face.

Eventually, I heard my name being called: "Angela."

"Yep," I said. "That's me."

Behind the curtain I went, into the emergency room. I was petrified. Fear of what might happen caused me to shake uncontrollably. I never fully understood why my dog shook so badly when I took her to the veterinary clinic. Now, I knew: she didn't know what they were going to do to her.

I was having a spaz attack. My involuntary muscles were twitching and spasming. I shivered like a girl standing out in the Arctic, naked as a jaybird.

## Your Guess Is as Good as Mine

A nurse came in to ask me questions and perform the standard procedures, such as taking my blood pressure. She asked if I had any allergies. I was coherent enough to know I was in the emergency ward; the sound of the ambulance siren only seemed to alarm me even more. I started convulsing.

"Get the doctor on the phone and tell him to get here now!" my mom called out. "She's getting worse."

When we heard Dr. Purina was on call that night, we all felt sick. "Crap," I mumbled as if auditioning for a ventriloquist role. "We might as well go to the vet clinic."

I'd been to see this doctor once and only once. I'd had an atrocious lesion on my lip, resembling a cold sore. It was utterly revolting, in a category all its own.

"Oh, she'll have that for life," Dr. Purina told my mom. "It'll never go away."

I was a teenager at the time. I burst into tears.

"I'll never get a date with this thing on my face!" I objected. "I might as well put a paper bag over my head and become a recluse."

Dr. Purina's best advice was to take an aspirin and my problem might go away... *eventually*. Mom reassured me she would take me to a different doctor. All's well that ends well, as they say. It turned out that the lesion disappeared in a few days with a prescribed topical cream.

Remembering this, I literally bit my lip (the one which supposedly would never heal) as Dr. Purina finally made his appearance. He asked me the same questions as the nurse. I was no further ahead. He assumed it must be epilepsy. Due to all my thrashing around, anyone would have been able to presume that diagnosis.

*Brilliant deduction, Doc,* I thought. *How did you arrive at that answer? I was flopping around like a chicken with its head cut off!*

He didn't know exactly what was wrong or what it could be. In fact, he had no solution to the problem. He left and went on his merry way; I imagine it was to watch a rerun of *ER*. Thanks for nothing.

Before he left the hospital grounds, he must have stumbled upon the idea that I should be monitored overnight. Obviously he thought I wasn't fit to go home. He decided I should be admitted, so up to the ICU I went. I had my own private nurse to keep a close eye on me at all times.

Then along came my worst enemy: intravenous.

"Here's an evening gown and robe to put on," the nurse politely said.

She worded it as though it were a lovely outfit to wear out on the town. I was in no mood to party. I was exhausted from doing the chicken dance; my wings had been flapping most of the night.

The last time I'd worn a robe was at karate class. If I'd been up to it, I could have used my self-defence training to kick the bag of fluid out of her reach. The "horse stance" came to mind, and I had a good mind to give the steel pole a karate chop—*hiya!* Get that thing away from my arm!

I had gone thirty-five years without any major incidents. I'd had a tonsillectomy back when I was a kid. As I recall, it had taken a half-dozen nurses to pin me down so they could put the IV in. I fought tooth and nail to escape those mean ladies in white.

They won.

## I Now Present to You… Alex

I asked Mom to contact Alex, my boyfriend. He had brown hair, hazel eyes, and super straight teeth. He seldom hid behind a smile and his dazzling white chicklets were his best feature. He strutted when he walked and was one of the most ambitious people I knew. Never wasting time, he was a real mover and shaker.

"We talk every night," I nervously said to Mom. "He's going to wonder why I'm not texting or answering his calls."

His job had him posted way up north, in Alberta. Seeing as he was working on the road, I knew he wouldn't be able to be there.

I lay there, wide awake. The heart monitor beeped constantly, annoying the heck out of me. Also accompanying me was the enemy—a long, slender steel pole filled with a saline solution to flush out anything and everything in my body. "Ivy" had obviously advanced to a higher level in karate, because she won the fight.

The nurse asked if I wanted to watch a movie. They had a terrible selection, but I chose one anyway. I hoped a flick might get my mind off my dilemma, but nope. I was a nervous wreck.

## I Plead: Not Guilty

My general practitioner came to visit bright and early the next morning. She asked a list of questions about what I thought might have triggered the incident. She prodded me for answers. It was like she was interrogating me, thinking I had taken some sort of illegal drugs. I was none too pleased about her accusations, as I'm proud to say I had never been high in my life. I'd suffer through a headache just so I didn't have to take something for it.

She persisted in her efforts to find out if I'd taken a drug someone had given me. She tried coaxing an answer out of me, saying my parents weren't here and not to worry about the outcome of their response. For the record, I was thirty-five years old; it's not like I was going to get grounded on account of bad behaviour. It was getting to the point where I was going to tell her I needed to talk to my lawyer. Case dismissed.

It turned out Mom had been beating herself up over the thought that maybe I was having a bad reaction to something she'd given me. I'd taken a swig of this new multivitamin drink she had ordered. When she came up to the hospital, the doctor (or the prosecutor) was still there. Mom told her she had given me a vitamin supplement in liquid form. Perhaps that was the culprit.

"What is this 'cocktail' you have given your child?" the doctor snapped. "I don't believe in all these herbal remedies." She knew nothing about the ingredients of this beverage. She scowled, snatched the suspect, read the label on the bottle, and handed it back to Mom.

Her questioning went nowhere. She told me she'd make an appointment with a neurologist. I was doing much better, though; no more shaking. My blood work came back and all appeared to be normal, so she sent me home.

For the first time in years, I missed a few days of work. I got home and snipped off my hospital wristband. I recuperated at home and it wasn't long before I felt normal again.

"It's all good," I said out loud, breathing a sigh of relief.

## Whiskers on My Chinny-Chin-Chin

The only other time I'd ever been in a hospital was following a minor incident in high school. Some jerk had decided it would be funny to stick his foot out and trip me. I was in a hurry and late for class, so I was taking big strides. I sprawled across the hallway and did a face plant right into the floor. My chin hit the hard surface and split open. Blood streamed down my neck; I must have looked like a vampire after a feeding.

I couldn't look in the mirror. I probably would have passed out at the thought of getting sutures. I grabbed a bunch of paper towels, but they didn't stop the bleeding. I ended up having to go up to the emergency room to get stitches, anyway.

After I got all fixed up, I returned to school with four black stitches sticking out of my chin. Like my day wasn't bad enough already, comments from the peanut gallery started coming at me like surround sound, but on different stations:

"Hey, Ang, did you forget to shave today?"

"What's up, Whiskers?"

"Here Kitty, Kitty!"

"Lost a catfight, eh?"

"You got a little something there."

You get the idea. It's a good thing I got rid of the hideous speed bump on my lip that Dr. Purina had said would be there for life. Imagine the material those cruel teenagers would have come up with:

"How *grows* it?"

"It's alive!"

"Nice knoll."

"Anyone feel like a round of golf? We can use Angela's face to tee off."

"Eww, gross! That infestation on your lip has swollen up like a tick."

## Laser Eye Surgery
*July 1998*

Being blind as a bat without wearing contacts or glasses, I decided to get laser eye surgery. Normally the term "surgery" freaks me out, but I knew this procedure didn't involve needles for freezing, so that appealed to me. I was oblivious, though, to the fact that I would be awake the whole time.

I remember the doctors putting drops into my eyes to numb them. My eyelids were held open with clamps to prevent blinking. I distinctly recall smelling what I'll describe as a "burnt hair smell."

*Oh my goodness,* I thought. *They're frying the cornea of my eye.*

The sizzling sound from the laser beams was a bit disturbing. I hated wearing glasses, though, so I sat through it. I couldn't wait to dispose of them in the drop box labelled "Old Glasses."

They gave me ginormous sunglasses which seemed to cover my whole face. When I took them off, the light was blinding. I felt like a newborn kitten opening its eyes for the first time.

I envisioned myself wearing a trenchcoat along with my enormous shades. I was, for the moment, Inspector Gadget. *I spy with my new, improved eyes, something that is...*

I took a gander in the mirror, only to say, "What big eyes you have! The better to see you with, my dear." I once was blind, but now I could see.

After the eye surgery, I had horrible night vision. Driving in the dark was annoying. My eyes were super sensitive, especially to the light of on-coming vehicles. The cars all seemed like they had their high beams on.

It was almost enough to turn me into a nocturnal creature. Even the moon didn't look the same. Imagine seeing a halo around a full moon—it's like a planet! I was constantly surrounded by halos, but to date I've never seen an actual angel.

I had to use eye drops to prevent infection. As I leaned my head back, I blinked like I'd been shot in the eye with a pea. Burn, baby, burn! I also used eye drops to keep them moist; they were dryer than the Sahara Desert, and at times I felt like I was standing in the middle of a sandstorm. But hey, during the day I was happy I wasn't near-sighted anymore.

## 20/20 Vision

I had perfect vision for awhile… until I noticed I kept rubbing my left eye; it didn't seem as clear as the right eye. During one of my follow-up appointments, the optometrist informed me that my left eye wasn't as crisp as the other.

I had been making payments on these peepers of mine, my eyes were under warranty, so to speak. Back then, being fairly new technology, I had forked out five grand and was going to see to it that I got my money's worth.

By November, I had to make another appointment, this time to get the left eye enhanced. I was annoyed because no one ever seems to get things right the first time. I had to go through the burnt hair experience again. I sat there, disappointed, as I smelt the singeing hair.

## Car Fanatics

I had met Alex not long before this whole schmozzle at the hospital. As far as I knew, I was healthy as a horse.

When the weekend arrived, so did Alex. There was an event going on in Weyburn called Cruise Night. The downtown area was blocked off and people came to show off their prized possessions. (Just so we're clear, I'm not talking about men showing off their trophy wives). It's a time when all car diehards get to shine and show their vehicles.

It was on this day that Alex and I expressed our mutual passion for muscle cars. As we walked around, he confessed that he owned a 1969 Camaro. I think he was surprised at my interest, as I drove a Sunfire. Woopty-doo.

He was intrigued when I told him about my very first car: a 1980 Trans Am. We spent the whole day oohing and aahing over cars. Afterward, we went back to my place and ordered pizza. He couldn't believe it when he noticed a car magazine on the coffee table. I could sense what he was thinking: *That's my girl, I know it!*

## You May Kiss the Bride
*March 2009*

And the two shall become one… Alex and I got married in Vegas. I wanted to keep things simple and stick to what I call the "get 'er done" ceremony. And no, Elvis did not marry us. Alex likes to tell people, "We didn't click on that option." The uniting took place at A Little White Chapel, located right on Las Vegas Boulevard. It has a 24-hour drive-up wedding window. Although Sin City never sleeps, we stuck with an afternoon ceremony. Just the two of us (the only ones invited) showed up… and that's the main thing.

On our way back to our hotel, being newlyweds, we stuck our heads out the limo's sunroof, looked at each, and screeched, "Ah!" We each looked at our left hand and realized we were officially off the market… game over. *Wah-wah.* Who does that, right? What a couple of weirdoes. No wonder we had to escape to Vegas to get hitched.

The first thing we did was hit a buffet. After filling our faces so much that we looked like pocket gophers, we carried the vote unanimously to go for a walk. We took a stroll, hand-in-hand, down the strip. We admired the architecture of the replicas of the world's most famous locales. My favourite was the Venetian, resembling Italy. It was so elaborate, with all its intricate details. The hotel even had perfumed air. From the moment

I walked into the casino, my nose was stuck so far into the air, I must have looked pompous.

"Alex, do you think we should go on a gondola ride?" I remarked at one point. My face must have resembled a shih tzu's, my bottom lip jutting out and my voice as high as the building itself. Seriously, the aroma in the hotel was intoxicating. It's worth a trip to Vegas just for the "smell of it."

We went to a mall and shopped. Weighed down with handbags on both arms, I carefully selected my favourite: a chocolate brown authentic Coach bag. Alex took it up to the front and watched as they wrapped it up in paper with the store's name and sticker. Along with the purchase came a dust bag to store the purse when it wasn't in use. I felt like I was keeping up with the Joneses. The purse was worth more than the money I had to put in it, but it's a wedding gift I'll always treasure.

From there, we found ourselves at a New York pretzel stand. We took our twisted treat and sat on a bench outside. I savoured the flavour, taking tiny bites between smiles. I reached for my sunglasses, looked at Alex, and exclaimed in my it-girl voice, "Man, would you look at the rockarossa on this *thang*!" My engagement ring was in new company, towering over seven other carats on a band of white gold with a row of glistening diamonds. Between the sun, my natural glow, and the shiny ring, it was bright out!

We burned off all the pretzel calories by walking countless blocks to Circus Circus. Alex and I sat down at a nickel machine and dropped some "beavers in the bucket" (Canadian slang). We selected a couple of slots, whirling around slowly on a carousel.

Alex seemed to be enjoying himself. The machine was like music to his ears as he swayed back and forth. I leaned over and said, "Must you rock? People are going to think you have autism."

After sitting on our fannies and not striking it rich, we picked up and left our silver behind. Evidently, we plunked our "heads or tails" coins into a lose/lose situation. Ah, well. Welcome to the city of Lost Wages!

We stumbled upon a Coke machine and I plopped in some chump change. Out came a Diet Coke, and I exclaimed, "Look, hon, I finally got me something. Here, now you try!" He slid some coins in and, sure as shooting, *ker-chunk,* he got a soda, too.

"This machine is hot!" I joked. "Should we keep playing, High Rolla?"

We took our winning soda pops and washed down a Krispy Kreme doughnut. "Yum yum in my tum tum," I said with a mouthful of carbs, rubbing my belly, which now stuck out like Buddha's.

I love to people watch, and let me tell you, you see all kinds in Vegas! The rich, the poor, and the very, *very* interesting are out and about at all hours. At one point, I had my observing glasses on and saw something out of the ordinary, like a sea creature on dry land. One particular man was seriously multitasking. Directly in front of him was a slot machine—his focal point—but like a couple of bodyguards, two other one-armed bandits flanked him. And as if the three machines weren't enough, he had another machine activated above.

"Hey, check out Squidly over there." I nudged Alex's arm and nodded my head in a two-o'clock direction.

Alex looked perplexed. "What in the world... I've never seen anything like it."

"That one's a true playa. Go for the gold!" I cheered from the sidelines.

"Huh. Olympic slots—only in Vegas," Alex muttered, shaking his head.

I was almost dizzy from watching the octopus in action. His Hawaiian button-up shirt looked like it was doing a hula dance of its own. He had a rhythm as he slapped the spin button directly in front of him. The next move was followed by his left hand, jutting out and hitting the repeat button. Move three was the right appendage reaching over and pushing the lit-up button. Lastly, he would reach up and tap the upper machine's magic button. Suddenly, one of his harems lit up and went berserk—*cha-ching*! All this commotion didn't even faze him.

"I do believe Octo-Man thinks of it as more of a job," I reckoned.

We left the aquatic squid show at his Sea World casino.

Speaking of water, our next adventure led us to the Bellagio, where we had tickets to see Cirque du Soleil. After the show, we watched the dancing waters outside the hotel and called it a night.

The next day, we visited a place where we met all kinds of celebrities. Without VIP passes, we got close enough to hear them breathe—but as real as they looked, they weren't breathing. We were at Madame Tussaud's wax museum. We used our imaginations and came up with different poses to keep the pictures interesting.

I caught up with Dwayne "The Rock" Johnson. I wasn't sure if he had his own bodyguards or if he just fended for himself. He was, after all, a professional wrestler, and his ring name said it best. Dwayne also acted in one of my favourite car movies, *Fast Five*.

The thing I love most about Vegas is all the lights. Tourists can travel the globe in one day! You can walk the strip and for a few minutes it's like you're in Europe. Then, on the way down the other side of the street, *boom*! You're in New York.

We didn't strike it rich in the city that never sleeps, but we didn't lose our shirts, either. No wonder Vegas is widely referred to as Sin City: tops, or lack thereof, seem to be the norm.

Time wasn't an issue. We kept the craziest hours, staying up super late and sleeping half the day away. By the time we got rolling each day, it was midafternoon. Lunch became our breakfast. Then we'd walk, walk, and walk some more, till the back of my heels screamed for mercy.

At the end of the trip, my blisters, my new husband, and all my shopping bags boarded the airplane. I'm sure I left a nose print on the window; my face was pushed against the glass, squinting, as I said farewell to the last hot rays of desert sun.

## Oh, to Be a Snowbird

I'm fascinated with palm trees. It's because they're considered tropical—unlike the trees that go through seasonal changes in Saskatchewan. There's nothing more depressing than staring out a window in the dead of winter and seeing a lifeless tree. Even Adam and Eve needed leaves. Palm trees, on the other hand, are always green; wherever there's year-long warm weather, one can find them.

I dread our long winters, so I brought some imposter palm trees into our house. It was the best I could do in our cold climate. The moral of the story is…you can't always get what you want. I'd love to live in a comfortable climate year-round, or at least get the heck out of here when the snow flies.

Alex always remembers to put a bug in my ear, though. "Any place that's hot has critters," he reminds me. I hate all insects. Whether I shudder over a cockroach or a less than tolerable winter, the thought of either made me shudder. I guess I have no choice but to choose the latter.

## Starting from Scratch

After getting married, my life changed drastically. I left everything I knew behind to move with Alex to Saskatoon. It was like looking in the rear-view mirror. I had to say adios to my family, friends, and work. I even had to part with clients; I'd built a relationship with them, and after nineteen years of cleaning, I mopped up the tears and moved on. I'm a creature of habit, so it wasn't easy for me to just pick up and leave.

I sold my house in Weyburn in 2008. Alex sold his place as well.

We soon came to the realization that our new house looked like Noah's Ark; after combining all our things, we had two of everything.

Angela Freriks

## Medical Alert
*February 2010*

For two years, I was symptom-free. That is, until…

Something happened. The first thing that crossed my mind was that I might be having a stroke. I felt the right side of my body weaken. Then my right hand began to have a tremor. I clenched it with my left, as if to hide the fact that it was happening. Sensing a dizzy spell coming on, I felt the need to sit. This episode only lasted for thirty seconds and I shook it off like a wet dog. I kept this to myself and went about my daily routine, feeling completely normal again.

A few days passed before it hit me again. It was the same unknown feeling. My right side was affecting my body's ability to function properly. This freakish occurrence only lasted about half a minute, and then it went away. Afterward, I was fine and went back to whatever I had been doing. I blew it off and denied there was anything wrong.

The problem reared its ugly head a third time while my parents were visiting one weekend. We were out and about, exploring Saskatoon, when I got in the back of the vehicle and sat there, stunned. I was weak on my right side, feeling faint, and my hand was twitching. Once again, this unwelcome situation resolved quickly. No one knew about my problem.

Two weeks later, I decided that I better go and get myself checked out. It was happening more frequently. Obviously something was wrong. A million thoughts rushed through my mind as to what the diagnosis could be. It could have been mini-strokes, Parkinson's, or MS. I drove myself mad trying to analyze it.

Of course, I didn't have a family doctor, having just moved to the city a few months earlier. I looked in the phonebook and decided on a medical clinic that had just opened in a new building close to where we lived. I asked if there was a female doctor who was taking new patients. Voilà, I was in.

## Monster Trucks

A fun event was planned for the coming weekend: a monster truck rally. Finally, a breath of fresh air! Well, far from it, actually. Our seats were fourth row from the arena and the exhaust fumes were thick. I love the smell of engines, especially diesel.

Our earplugs were in place, but the roaring engines were still really loud. One monster truck totally crushed the cars it ran over, leaving the arena in a cloud of dust. The stadium was full of fans waving checkered flags; others were shoving fists full of popcorn in their faces. The noise level was like a mix between Chuck E. Cheese, a factory, and a racetrack.

After the big trucks, motocross bikes hit the track sounding like a swarm of mosquitoes. The riders flew into the air after jumping mounds of dirt, leaning their agile bodies to get around tires and pylons, racing to the finish line. My eyes stung from all the fumes.

The last event was the demolition derby. Cars deliberately smashed into each other, creating more than mere fender benders. One particular car took the most abuse, getting bumped and bruised beyond belief; the engine eventually started on fire and it was toast. We were seated so close that I found myself closing my eyes, worried that something might fly off and head in our direction.

When we returned home, our clothes smelled like a carburetor. We were practically deaf and dirty all over. When I cleaned out my ears with a Q-tip, the ends came out black. Next, I blew my nose; the tissue looked like a dust rag. Alex said his Kleenex had looked like an oil change rag.

## Vertigo

*March 2010*

Not knowing who was going to open the door to the room, I was a bit on edge. I nervously flipped through a magazine as I waited for our meet and greet. The woman who eventually greeted me had an above-average build. Her accent was as thick as her waistline and I struggled to understand her broken English—and it was pertinent that I understand every word.

The woman introduced herself as Dr. Hicks; at least, that's what I called her, as her long last name was hardly repeatable. When I asked how to say her name, she jumbled all the letters together. I came to the conclusion that my brain didn't have the capacity to absorb all those syllables.

She commented that I was a nice lady. I found this odd, as she didn't know me from a hole in the ground. However, I proceeded to tell her my troubles and strange symptoms, including my lightheaded dizzy spells. She didn't say anything, instead clicking away at the keyboard.

"When was your last physical?" she finally asked. "We need to do a complete physical. I'll send you for blood work." More clicking. "So, tell me, are you married?" Then, in the next breath, "Do you have children?"

*Not that question again, for the love of… That question got asked every time I met someone new.*

"No, I don't have any children," I replied shortly, but not rudely.

"Are you on birth control pills?"

"No."

"Then you want to get pregnant?"

"Me? Not so much." I knew she could read my body language quite clearly. "No, absolutely not. That's the farthest thing from my mind."

Dr. Hicks raised an eyebrow. "You are thirty-seven years old and you have no babies?" She spoke to me like I was a rare case and I'd sell on eBay for big bucks. Next, she asked if I wanted to come in and talk about the possibility of having a child. Was she for real? She told me we could discuss the pros and cons, and the risk factors due to my age (since I was apparently an old fossil). At this point I was annoyed, thinking she might have to recheck my blood pressure.

*Pregnancy is the last thing on my to-do list,* I thought, annoyed.

"So, do you have any inkling as to what this thing I described could be?" I blurted out. "Do you think I have Parkinson's?"

"No" would have been a good answer. Instead, she said, "I shouldn't say anything until our next visit and I get the results back from your physical examination. But I would suspect it's epilepsy."

"What? Are you serious?" My eyes felt like they were as wide as saucers. I'm pretty certain my voice cracked. I thought an epileptic was someone who had grand mal seizures and lost consciousness. I had ruled it out; I knew exactly what was going on around me and I never ended up on the floor with major convulsions.

"There are many kinds of epilepsy," she explained. "Yours would be considered mild, if that's what it is. I don't know for sure. Come back and see me." She ended our conversation with, "It was very nice to meet you. You are a lovely girl."

*Don't you mean I'm an old dinosaur with epilepsy and no children?*

I left the clinic with a sad puppy dog face. I got in my vehicle and immediately my eyes stung, my lips quivered, and the waterworks began. I couldn't hold back the tears as I sat in a hazy stupor.

I tossed aside the sheet with all the checkmarked boxes.

"I'm not going for blood work today," I said like the strong-willed child I was. Those bloodthirsty vampires were going to have to wait. I despised needles!

Not knowing what my health issue could be was driving me around the bend, but I still managed to keep my hands on the wheel, although the tears obstructed my view. The heavy downpour continued all the way home.

I headed straight for the computer and pulled up a YouTube video of a song called "Bad Day," by Daniel Powter. Misery loves company, and the co-pilot was just another sad song. I sounded like a cat caught in a fan belt; I sounded so terrible, I darn near made my own ears bleed.

I leaned forward, put my elbows on the desk, and cupped my chin in the palms of my hands. The video became a blur. I sat in the house, all by my lonesome, and had a pity party. At that point, I didn't know what to do.

My lips quivered as I endured a one-on-one conversation with myself: "But I just traded my life for a new one. I left my hometown behind. I just got married and was counting on being on cloud nine, but instead…"

I climbed into bed, curled up into a fetal position, and bawled my eyes out. I felt sorry for myself. The transition in my life had been overwhelming. I was in a strange city and didn't know anyone except my husband. I missed my old surroundings and wished a friend would come over and comfort me.

Most of all, I missed my "mommy," who had always been there for me in whatever bad situation came my way. There's just something about a mother/daughter relationship. A special bond must develop during the nine months of pregnancy, a bond that grows stronger over time. I used to see Mom practically every day. Either she would come over (usually with food) or I'd stop in for a visit at my parents' house.

Then I thought about my dear ol' friend, my German shepherd. We'd had to say our final goodbyes on account of her old age. Thank goodness for my dog's big ears, which I don't think she ever fully grew into. She hadn't had a choice but to become a good listener. That dog of mine heard it all. If she'd been my therapist, I would have had a hefty bill to pay after twelve years of loyal listening. She was always there for me and not once did she cancel a session. We'd go for walks together and I'd take her out to the field to run free. I'd vent as I scratched her ears and she'd grunt as if she understood me. Through her seemingly sad brown eyes, she showed compassion. The best part was that her lips were always sealed. Anything and everything I told her remained a secret. I think that's why dogs are referred to as "man's best friend."

I sure did miss that old girl and really wished she was around so I could give my compadre a big hug.

My husband returned home from work. It would've been normal had I been mopping, but instead I was moping around the house. He could tell by my grave expression that something was wrong.

"Why the long face?" he dared ask.

I described the events at the doctor's office and told him that she thought I had epilepsy.

Pause.

"And check this out," I continued, with my hand in the air. My neck looked like a cobra, swaying from side to side. "She had the audacity to say, 'Thirty-seven and no babies?' Sheesh! Like I really want to be barefoot and prego. I don't want a bun in the oven."

Alex shook his head and immediately had a bewildered look on his face. After an awkward silence, he asked, "What's that all about? It doesn't make sense."

"My sentiments exactly," I scorned. "What a moron…"

Alex threw out the word "Imbecile" like it was a hardball and I should take another swing.

"No doubt," I said. "I'm only sticking with her because she's a female doctor. Being a lady and all, I'd have expected to have a better experience during the pap test. That was the most brutal examination I've ever had. She scraped the cells off like she was peeling heavy snow off the driveway."

I cringed, then exhaled.

We stood up from the table and I wrapped my arms around my next of kin, hugging him like I was a koala bear.

I felt bad for Alex. After all, we'd only been married eleven months. We should still have been experiencing heavenly bliss, not worrying about storm clouds.

Angela Freriks

## Just a Little Poke

A week went by and my mother asked how everything was going. I pursed my lips and confessed that I hadn't done the bloodletting thing yet. She told me I better go and get it over with.

"Yeah, yeah. When I'm good and ready," was my solemn vow.

I psyched myself up enough to face Dracula. I walked up to the front desk of the clinic like I was heading to the principal's office. I grabbed a number and sat down. When my number was called, the girl was eager to get to work.

"I'm looking for some nice, big juicy veins," she said.

Then I was escorted to Room #2, where I involuntarily found myself staring into space. I rolled up my sleeve and out came the rubber hose to tie around my arm. And then the needle.

"Just a poke now and it'll all be over," the girl reassured me.

I stared at a picture of a palm tree that was right in front of me. Feeling the blood drain from my arm, I quickly found a seat-sale and envisioned myself on a tropical island.

*Get me out of here. This vision of palm trees is a farce.*

"You can go now," the flight attendant said.

Back to reality. *You did well and you need a reward,* I told myself. *Go get yourself a doughnut.*

Good work always involves reward. After all, my dog always got a treat for good behaviour.

## Rattle My Nerves
### *April 2010*

Dr. Hicks must have figured my situation was urgent, since she took the liberty of contacting a neurologist. Normally, one would have to wait quite a while to see a specialist, but she got the ball rolling.

I sat in the neurologist's office, a nervous wreck, my eyes scoping the room. I wasn't comfortable with my surroundings, which weren't pleasing to the eye. The walls were decorated in posters of disturbing art about stroke symptoms and 3D muscle tissue. I wanted to look outside, but the drapes were closed. There wasn't a magazine in sight.

With a firm handshake, I soon met the doctor, who I'll call Dr. Neurotron. He took a seat on his stool against a backdrop of beige filing cabinets. He wore a white lab coat and had a stethoscope around his neck.

I told him of the sporadic muscle spasms in my right hand and weakness in my right leg. I stammered as I continued, feeling a weird but warm sensation throughout my body. I was usually cold and wore pull-over bunny hugs, but lately I had resorted to hoodies with a zipper. That way when I suddenly felt hot, I could unzip it.

Dr. Neurotron listened with the utmost curiosity as I climbed onto the examination table. First he took his tiny flashlight and did a "spot-check test" in my eyes, checking left, then right. I assumed he was looking for evidence of a stroke. This was followed by him holding up his fingers and asking me how many fingers I saw; I assumed he was testing my peripheral vision. Then he took a toothpick and poked me with it, as if I was a cake fresh out of the oven. He hammered on my knee and I almost kicked him, an involuntary reflex.

"Reflexes are good," he exclaimed.

I was still sitting on the examination table, my feet dangling, when he bent down and slipped my socks off. He then grabbed another metal instrument off his table and ran it along the bottom of my foot. I have the most ticklish feet, so I squirmed and giggled at the same time. Along came another cold, steel tool which he held against my hands and feet. It buzzed and he wanted to know if I could feel it. I could. I stood up and he checked my balance while I closed my eyes.

After the check-up, he cross-examined my story to confirm what had actually occurred during the episode. I insisted that I remained conscious and never blacked out. That's when it dawned on me that I had been taking a nasal decongestant. Perhaps that had caused these side effects.

He sat on his stool, pondering for a moment, then came up with the same answer as my family doctor. "I'm not exactly sure what this could be. I suspect it's epilepsy as well. I want to send you for some blood tests so I can further assess the problem. This should be done as soon as possible. Contact my office if your condition worsens and I'll treat you for epilepsy. I'll write you out a prescription, if need be."

I walked out of his office. Before leaving, I turned back, stopping him before he disappeared into the file room behind the desk.

"Are you sure this doesn't have anything to do with the nasal spray?" I asked impatiently.

"No, that's not it."

He wasn't going to medicate me, since he didn't know for sure if it was epilepsy, even though that was his prognosis.

*It must be the nose spray I've been snorting,* I told myself, in denial that it could be anything worse. I was discouraged yet again, as now even a specialist didn't know what was wrong with me. I made up my mind to dump the bottle of nasal decongestant down the drain.

## Hi-ho, Hi-ho—Off to the Clinic I Go

I told myself to suck it up and go back to the bloody clinic (pardon the pun). Chances were good they still had me on the computer and I wouldn't have to go through the withdrawal procedure again.

I walked up to the desk. "I was in here not long ago. Here's the form the neurologist gave me."

She looked the form over. "It looks like he wants a few different tests done. We'll send them to the hospital and they'll report back to the neurologist."

"Okay," I sulked. I hung my head like a disappointed child who wasn't getting her way. "Let's get this over with."

"Not today, though." the nurse said. She informed me that one of the tests required fasting, so I had to come back early another morning, having had no liquids or food.

Did she have any idea what she was asking of me? Fasting. I had never fasted in my life. I ate every two hours, it seemed. I was all about food. The thought of not having coffee at breakfast was just wrong; it was my motivation to get out of bed in the morning. Breakfast was my favourite meal of the day. I'd eat pancakes, toast, cereal, or a muffin three times a day if I could.

## Oh No, You *Dit-ten*

In 2006, I met a guy and agreed to go out for supper with him as friends. When the waitress came around after the meal, she asked if we cared for dessert. He was so stuffed that he said, "Oh, no thanks, I'm too full."

I knew the dessert was included with his meal, and this restaurant had the best rice pudding one could imagine. Normally I was an introvert and didn't say too much, but my salivary glands had other ideas. It was all I could do to refrain from giving this fellow a good swift kick under the table. Too full? There was no such thing. That was as preposterous as declining money, as if being *too* rich was even possible.

I barely knew this poor lad, but I couldn't help but voice my opinion. After the waitress left, I bluntly told him, "For the record, you *always* want dessert!"

He looked at me like I was off my rocker. "Should I call the waitress back so you can have my dessert?"

I'd made a total fool of myself, acting as though I'd fallen off the wagon of an overeaters anonymous support group. Almost being deprived of this dessert had brought out assertiveness I never knew I had. Even though the moment was awkward, I shovelled in the rice pudding; he ate a mint.

Angela Freriks

## Blood Banking

I got up—no coffee, no breakfast, not even a stick of gum. I was behind the wheel, doing my Count Dracula impersonation, "I vant to suck your blood: one vial… *Ah, ah, ah…* two vials."

Déjà vu. The girl escorted me back to Room #2. I saw the same palm tree; what were the odds? I guess it was time for me to pretend I was in… Palm Springs, I decided.

"Arm up on the table and clench your fist, please," I heard the lady say.

*Oh, you wanna arm wrestle, lady?* my inner voice wisecracked.

I sensed she was holding her weapon of choice. Next, she chose her target—that poor undeserving vein, the brave one that stood up and said, "Pick me; I'll do it." Then it was punctured and tortured like it knew something but wasn't at liberty to say… Injection! And it was pierced with a pointed object. One vein actually collapsed on the scene.

"All done," she said, holding a cotton swab against the dark hole. She added a band-aid on top.

All right, free to go. I was just as excited to get out of there as one is to get out on bail. First things first: I needed to get some coffee pumping through my veins.

Deciding to take the band-aid off, I remembered that the quick and painless method might be best. I ripped it off and yelled, "Yeow! Dag nabbit." The skin around the inside of my elbow was as tender as a rose. I never had any problem waxing my own eyebrows, but when it came to needles my pain tolerance was low.

## Straining My Eyes

My eyes didn't seem as good as they once were. I struggled with reading street signs and menus that were mounted to walls. My eyesight seemed to be failing. I had been told when I had laser eye surgery that when I got to be around forty, I might need glasses again, but just for reading. At the time, I thought, *That doesn't apply to me because I don't read.*

What next? I had enough going on. I thumbed through the Yellow Pages and pointed my finger to a nearby optometrist.

As I sat in the waiting room, I wondered if the first letter on the eye chart was still "E." It had been quite a few years since I'd had my eyes examined.

I sat in a room and the girl told me to put my chin and forehead against a piece of equipment. I remember staring at a red barn when suddenly I felt a puff of air shoot into my eye. My whole body shook, I jumped back, and I nearly fell backwards out of my chair.

"Sorry about that," she said as though I hadn't so much as flinched. "You blinked, so we're going to have to redo it."

"Hokey smokes! You could at least warn a person!" I snapped, somewhat stunned.

I guess I should have realized something was up, as prior to the exam she'd put drops in my eyes to dilate the pupils. I figured she was testing me for glaucoma, but I didn't hear it from her.

She ditched me, which didn't hurt my feelings, and introduced me to the optometrist. I had a bad feeling.

The doctor gave me a black plastic stick and told me to cover my left eye. I couldn't believe what I saw—or didn't see, rather. I had hoped to at least get some of the letters right, but to be perfectly honest, I think I had an easier time when I was in kindergarten. Obviously, I failed miserably with the other eye, too, as I heard these words: "Here's your prescription. We have a large selection of glasses in the front. One of the girls will gladly help you pick out a pair."

I sat there in a catatonic state. It took me a minute before I spoke.

"Glasses?"

The question was more for me than for her. My eyes had gone back to the way they'd been back in 1998. I was near-sighted again. I didn't need reading glasses, but regular, everyday glasses. I was madder than a hatter. I considered my beautiful blue eyes to be my best feature, but now I had to hide them behind lenses—again.

## EEG

*May 2010*

My cell phone rang and displayed an unknown number. I flipped it open to discover that it was the hospital calling. The neurologist had set up an appointment for me to have an EEG (electroencephalogram).

"Sorry," I said. "I'm at work and you caught me off guard. What hospital is this and what is this regarding? Where, what time, and what sort of test is this?"

"Maybe you better write this down," the woman said. "Do you have a pen and paper handy?"

I scrambled for something to write on and scribbled down her words. "I'm new to the city and there are three hospitals, so which one do I go to?" I asked, in panic mode.

"Can you make the appointment at RUH?"

"Yes, I'll be there."

"Okay, now we need you to have clean hair."

I furrowed my brow. She must have known I was perplexed.

"What I mean is, have your hair shampooed, thoroughly combed," she continued. "And no hairspray. It's a test where we put electrodes on your head."

On the actual day of this freaky-deaky test, I wasn't in a calm state. I finally stumbled upon a parking spot and got the ticket stub system figured out. I found my way to the admitting desk, although I wasn't planning to stay.

I decided I better hit the whizzer first. I walked into the washroom and just about said, "Trick or treat!" The stalls were yellow and orange, the toilet white. The vanity was bright orange.

*Will wonders never cease…*

I suddenly had a hankering for candy corn. That morning, I had applied some candy corn lip balm from Avon. I wasn't much of an Avon lady, but I'd ordered three different flavoured lip glosses for Halloween season.

At last, I managed to locate the laboratory. I figured I should call it a lab, for obvious reasons: laboratory had the word *rat* in it!

The lady running the test had a soothing voice and I liked her pleasant personality right from the get-go. She explained everything she was going to do and reassured me that nothing would hurt. She sectioned my hair into several parts, then slopped this cold goop on my scalp and proceeded to slap on suction cups. I had a great abundance of wires hanging from my head. I felt like a squid in an electric chair, tentacles in disarray.

She sent me over to another table where she hooked me up to a machine to measure my brain's electrical activity. Her next instructions were for me to lie down on a hospital bed. For starters, she turned off all the lights, except for one—a strobe light. I thought my eyes were playing tricks on me as the lamp flashed. It was like psychedelic images from the 80s. In the background I heard different sounds: a piano, a piccolo, and some chirping—birds, I figured—birds, tickling the ivories. I had no idea. It was like a kaleidoscope of different shapes and colours, creating abstract art, a kind of strange hallucination in which distortions came towards me in 3D. My mind swirled around, in a blinding snowstorm with enormous flakes mixed with food colouring. My eyelids were so heavy, my eyes so traumatized from the brightness that I felt tears drip down.

She claimed that lots of people, especially kids, fell asleep during this exam… so I was to just relax. As I lay on the table, the room still lacking overhead lights, she said she was going to leave. I assured her I wouldn't fall asleep, for a few reasons. For one, I'd never been taught how to relax; it wasn't in my vocabulary. Secondly, I'd never even fallen asleep during a movie! And I'm not a calm person, especially with not understanding these machines or the peculiar thingies on my cranium.

She re-entered after being gone a short time. Hearing her walk in, I said, in a juvenile tone, "I'm not sleeping."

I had to do another strange test and breathe like I'd been running for a long period of time. I felt like a chimpanzee swinging from branch to branch, lost in the jungle. Hyperventilating, I could empathize with asthmatics.

As one of my passions in life, I used to participate in five- and ten-kilometre runs. I even trained for a half-marathon. In September 2005, I ran in the Queen City Marathon. I'm proud to say I completed this daunting task in two hours, fifteen minutes. I did everything in my power to focus on the finish line, even though my legs felt like jello. What a joyful day, and one of the greatest accomplishments of my life. At the end of the race, a medallion was placed around my neck. Mission complete.

As my mind went back in time, I envisioned the nurse being my pace bunny; she kept telling me I was doing great. The whole point of the test was to measure electrolytes. I felt like yelling, "Bring it on! Now's the time to present yourself." I was hoping for my hand to twitch so the test could measure the abnormal activity.

I wasn't able to wrap my brain around the whole idea, but the nurse was. My head was bandaged up and I must have looked like King Tut. Now even this lady was trying to make me a "mummy." People, please, not every woman on the planet must bear children.

After the test was all said and done, she gently pulled the conglomeration of wires from my head and tried to comb through my rat's nest. When I went to the washroom, my hair looked like I'd stuck my head in a deep fryer. I asked the grease monkey in the mirror if she wanted fries with her wrap. I left the hospital with the grimiest hair you ever did see.

## What's Up, Doc?

Now for the results. When I went back to see Dr. Hicks, the EEG results turned out to be normal. She announced this without emotion. So, both the specialist and my family doctor were still unable to pinpoint my problem. My case needed further investigation. Dr. Neurotron suggested that I get an MRI.

I watched *ER* every Thursday evening, but I never actually thought I'd have to be in one of those MRI machines. While surfing the web, I clicked on a picture of one, talking like a surfer stoked at catching a wave, "Whoa, totally tubular, dude."

I didn't know what MRI stood for until I looked it up on the computer: magnetic resonance imaging. They're used to scan patients and provide physicians with detailed images and specific diagnostic information. An MRI machine is a safe diagnostic procedure that uses a magnetic field and radio waves to create detailed images of the body. MRI machines involve magnets, which may interact with metal to distort the image. The exam is a painless procedure and is noninvasive, without the use of X-rays or other radiation.

I chuckled to myself and figured the machine would be dead set against any heavy metal playing through my headphones. It would frown upon me listening to Iron Maiden, Led Zeppelin, or Metallica. And guys, lose the "I'm all that" attitude; this machine doesn't like so-called "chick magnets."

Rules: No snaps, no shoes, no scan!

I received a call from the MRI department and asked to be put on a short-call list. I informed the woman on the phone that I lived in the city and could be there within a half-hour if there was ever a cancellation. After answering a ton of questions about my health, she also asked if I was claustrophobic and if I could lie still for thirty minutes to an hour and a half. That's quite a time difference—a half-hour I could do, hopefully, but I didn't know about anything longer.

Angela Freriks

## Shut Your Pie Hole

Unless you're in the medical field and know facts for sure, button your lip. For example, when I told someone that I had to get an MRI, the less than knowledgeable person said, "Oh no, you have a tattoo; the ink has lead in it and it will be painful."

My pain tolerance is less than nil. I have no idea how or why, for that matter, I sat through the painful procedure of getting a tat done in the first place. I was seventeen years old when my friend and I decided to get matching tattoos. Technically, you have to be eighteen to get ink done, or have your parents' permission. Well, what can I say, we were scoundrels back then. But your sins will find you out. When my dad noticed a rose on my ankle (classic, I know), he didn't think it was real.

"I sure hope that washes off," he said in a disapproving tone.

"It's a real tatty, Daddy."

I must've been brain-dead back in high school. The tattoo artist gave me rules, which I broke. He told me to stay out of the sun and keep out of the pool. Nay. It was summer holidays and I wasn't going to hide behind the clouds, nor was I going to be confined to dry land. My friend with the matching tattoo joined me in the hot sun, and of course we were in the pool, with chlorine—which made our poodle hair look even frizzier.

Due to our disobedience, our roses began to fade; the petals were withering. Stupid flowers—they don't last long. My brave friend told me she was going to get hers recolored and asked me if I wanted to get mine redone, too. I didn't even have to think about it. Not a chance! The heck with that procedure; she was on her own. I wasn't going to go through the pricking of a needle gun on my skin again. Getting a tattoo is like a cat scratching you over and over—and yeah, you bleed.

Cranium Crisis

## Quit Rocking the Boat
*June 2010*

Not much time passed before I was asked if I could be at St. Paul's Hospital in half an hour. I was just about to have lunch at the time, so I wolfed down my sandwich and punched the location into the GPS. Thankfully I had it with me, since I had no clue where to go. I followed the voice-activated gadget and listened intently to the instructions.

Needless to say, I was a bundle of nerves. The staff was polite. This was my first experience heading into the large doughnut-shaped magnet and I was frightened about the pain I'd been forewarned about because of the tattoo. The man doing the screening questions told me that in rare cases ink could affect the machine, and if so they would pull me out.

I proceeded to lie down on the firmly padded table. Thank goodness they provided headphones to make it a little more tolerable. They asked me what radio station I wanted to listen to. *Right on, I love listening to music. It helps pass the time quickly.* The girl put the headphones on me and asked if I wanted a blanket. I figured I needed the extra covers because I was always cold and this was no time to shiver. I felt like I needed a Linus blanket, but didn't want to act like a baby. Through the headphones, I could hear her voice describe that I would be subjected to a lot of loud noises and I'd have to lie perfectly still or they'd have to do it over again.

My mind raced, as well as my heart; it was a tossup as to which would reach the finish line first. In my left hand was a "help" buzzer, which I thought of as a panic button. I hoped I wouldn't involuntarily squeeze it due to, well, panic. I wanted to get out of there ASAP.

A hundred and one things ran through my mind. I wondered about the circumference of the cylinder. I thanked my lucky stars that I wasn't a large person, or else I might have felt like I was stuck in the trunk of an Austin Mini.

I played the broken record of the what-if game over and over: *What if I get itchy and need to scratch? What if I develop an involuntary twitch?*

*What if I need to cough or sneeze? What if it feels like there's something in my eye—an eyelash, perhaps? What if I have to whiz, or worse yet, flatulate? What if they can read what I'm thinking?*

My biggest concern was being able to lie still. I was always so restless and fidgety.

"Don't move or I'll shoot," I said to myself. All of a sudden, Elmer Fudd's voice encouraged me to stay calm: "Be vewy, vewy still when hunting pwoblums."

The voice was interrupted by a knocking sound from somewhere in the circular area of the long tube. Then I heard a horrible sound. It was like an engine that wouldn't turn over in the dead of winter. The machine jolted, like the annoying person sitting behind you in a theatre, kicking your seat.

Inside the culvert-like contraption, I tried to keep my mind occupied. I imagined myself to be having a rejuvenating experience, taking advantage of an all-day spa gift package. Perhaps I was in an aqua bed; I'd never had an aqua massage, but I pretended this was what it would be like. I told myself that all the thumping noises were just jets of water working the knots out of my tense body. Getting an MRI probably wasn't cheap, so I imaged that I was an A-list celebrity, spending a huge wad of cash on a super deluxe machine.

With every passing minute, I wondered what was happening to my body in this machine. The volume was intense; it sounded like there were bullets ricocheting off the inside of the MRI machine. *Pa-tink! Pa-ting! Pa-chew!* Take cover! Then, from out of nowhere, a machine gun started firing rounds. *Ddddrrr! Bddd! Dddrrr*! It would have been an automatic reaction to cover my ears, but I already had the headphones on. I shouted in my mind, "Cease fire! Drop your weapons. I demand silence!" The racket continued, with shots being fired from, I'm guessing, an Uzi or an AK-47. *Rat-a-tat-tat! Da da da da!*

My heart pounded with an abnormal rhythm and I felt like I needed to get out of there. Maybe I should have taken a sedative. I knew there was no pain involved; it was the emotional pain of not knowing what might be wrong with me.

I tried imagining myself inside a tanning bed, soaking up the solar rays. I was having a fake-and-bake session and my minutes were almost up. The fact remained, though, that I was in this confined space for a reason... but what was it?

If this wasn't over soon, I was going to have to press the button and get out of this closed casket. I felt trapped and antsy.

The girl's voice interrupted the song and the hammering stopped. "We're going to pull you out now."

*Oh, thank goodness.*

"The doctor has requested we put in an IV and inject a dye, so the radiologist can get a clear view and a better analysis," she said. "The gadolinium-based compound highlights scans to enhance the specific area. You may feel a cool/warm sensation in your arm."

I was glad she pulled me out of the machine. If she would have told me while I was still inside, I would have wanted to sit up straight and barter with her. My instincts would've been to hit the button because when my veins got wind they were going to be interrogated, again, they throbbed nervously. It was like the blood started to boil; my veins were mad, as was I. First the blood clinic wanting to poke and prod me, and now these evil creatures want to insert an IV. This was a needle and it would stay in! This unwanted visitor wasn't at all welcome, but banged on the door anyway, eager to inflict more pain...

"I'm going to inject the solution now," the girl said, her voice somewhat sympathetic. "This is a pediatric syringe, so it's the smallest one."

My body moaned with pity, trying to feel more at ease. I felt cold liquid course through my veins, making its way up my arm.

"We're going to put you back in for about fifteen minutes," she informed me.

So, I slid back into the tunnel of turbulence and told myself, *I guess I have to do what I have to do. Let's get this thing over with.*

Finally, after what sounded like visiting a construction site, she pulled me out. I got out of that doughnut hole faster than a cat in a bath.

*  *  *

I had to strain to understand Dr. Hicks, but thankfully she printed off a sheet from Dr. Neurotron. The letter went something like this:

> I saw Angela in consultation, presenting with symptoms of a partial motor seizure. Her neurological examination was normal. I felt that the symptoms were consistent with a seizure of front temporal origin, left side.
>
> A brain MRI was obtained, which confirms the presence of a left cerebral hemispheric tumour, measuring 1.4 x 5.5 x 2.3 cm, with associated mild mass effect encompassing the left cingulated gyrus. The reporting radiologist indicates that the lesion is most consistent with the diagnosis of an epidermoid.
>
> I would recommend initiating this patient on treatment with an anticonvulsant regimen; I would suggest treatment with Keppra (Levetiracetam), combined with a multivitamin, folate, and vitamin D.
>
> Yours sincerely,
> Dr. Neurotron

## Coconut in My Coconut

I stopped at a bakery one day, giving in to a craving. I had a sweet tooth for baklava. I had trouble digesting the phrase, "You have a brain tumour," and upon hearing the description of it, I felt the same way about the baklava. When I went to the fridge, I had every intention of devouring this tasty treat. But as I looked down at the baklava roll, my stomach churned.

I noticed the top was covered in coconut. The stringy strands stuck out in all directions. I imaged it to be the tumour, covered with tiny hair follicles. That's when I reached in the drawer, grabbed a ruler, and measured every dimension of the dessert. The dimensions of the piece of baklava measured exactly, to the millimetre, the dimensions of the tumour.

For the first time in my life, I can honestly say I lost my appetite. There was no way I could eat it. I was in such shock. I took a photo of the baklava with my cell phone and another snapshot with my camera. I wrapped it up and was dry-heaving as I put it back in the fridge. I'm not sure why I didn't fling it across the room or immediately throw it in the trash, but I wanted to show my husband this deduction. I thought he might be intrigued.

With him, everything had to be measured to a tee and be perfectly in line. I'm thankful I had braces when I was younger; had I not, when I first met him, one smile with crooked teeth would've been a red flag. When he got home, he confirmed that the measurements were bang on. Alex would eat everything, though— to my knowledge, there isn't one food or drink he doesn't like. Despite my story, he proceeded to consume the baklava, one tiny morsel at a time.

## Overreact Like a Hypochondriac

I searched the internet for different epilepsy medications. I tried to educate myself, but in doing so I was sickened by one story in particular. I read that one's gum line can grow over one's teeth, requiring gum surgery. I didn't want to have a dentist reconstruct my gums. Nasty!

At my next dentist appointment, I queried the dental hygienist about certain medications having horrific outcomes. I was in freak-out mode and begged her to tell me my gums were normal. She indicated they were fine, but out of the blue, she came out with, "Are you bulimic?"

She had the metal mirror and pick in my mouth and I felt like a fish on a hook. I looked at her, my eyes as big as a blowfish, mumbled, and blew up a spit bubble.

"Huh?"

"The reason I'm asking is because of the deterioration on your teeth. Any acid can cause enamel erosion. May I suggest that you get an over-the-counter prescription for acid reflux? I'm also going to suggest you get a fluoride treatment each time you come in."

She was long-winded. I opened and closed my mouth till my jowls hurt; I had no choice but to lie there and listen as she poked around, wiping plaque off her pick and onto my apron.

I wasn't happy about her allegations. I was carrying around a belly full of carbs, but what I scarfed down the hatch wasn't coming back up the hatch. I certainly didn't have bulimia.

## The Final Straw

I remember having concerns and questions for Dr. Hicks and wanting to know what the next step would be. I must have been her last patient before noon because she seemed very eager to get me out of her office. She was short with me when I asked about the possibility of needing surgery and how long the recovery period would be. I asked her about complications and risk factors. She explained that another patient of hers had just gone through surgery and had come out fine. She went on to tell me that it was a simple procedure and not to worry.

On my way in, I noticed a sign taped to the door stating that Dr. Hicks was leaving and her last day would be at the end of the month. I asked her why she was leaving.

My jaw dropped when I heard her cold words. "You're the reason I'm leaving."

I sat there in disbelief. It took me a minute to absorb whether or not I'd heard her correctly. I couldn't believe she would have the nerve to say such a thing, at such an extremely unfortunate situation. I wasn't looking for sympathy, just a little compassion. When I'd first met her I thought she was pleasant and doing her best to treat me. I wish I would've had her words recorded.

I told her my meds didn't seem to be helping and I was still experiencing symptoms. She immediately started typing out a prescription to double up on the medication. I told her I wasn't comfortable with doubling up, due to the potential side effects. She wouldn't listen to me. Thank goodness for my husband's drug plan, as it was costing a pretty penny already.

"We are doubling the dosage," she insisted. She scribbled her illegible signature on the prescription pad and left the chicken scratching on her desk. She abruptly got up from her chair. "Now, come back and see me again if this doesn't help."

Without saying another word, she walked out the door.

I grumbled about what to say to her, but nothing came out. What I wanted to scream was, "I don't want your autograph; I'm the furthest thing from your biggest fan right now! Enjoy your lunch, Hungry, Hungry Hippo! And for the record, I'm now thirty-eight and there's still no embryo, no ultrasound is needed, nope, nothing in my belly… just a cesspool of distress."

The whole incident threw me for a loop. I exited the office and tried to contain myself. I shut the door to my vehicle and bawled; a dam couldn't have held back my tears.

*I'm the reason she's leaving,* kept spinning around in my head like a broken record. *I bid you adieu, so long, I'm gone. That's it; our relationship is so over! Yeah, this thing we've got going on here, it isn't working. You and me, Hicks…we're done. Finito. It's you, not me!*

Maybe it was a mutual agreement. She'd told me I was the reason she was leaving, but to my knowledge I hadn't done anything wrong. In my opinion, Dr. Hicks lacked common sense. Why would Alex and I consider starting a family at such a crucial time? With a major health scare, MRIs, medication… seizures! It wouldn't be fair to the baby.

The search was on to find a new lady doctor. I checked numerous medical clinics, but not one of them was accepting new patients. No biggie. I didn't need a doctor that bad. It was just a scratch… right?

Wrong.

I decided to go back to the same clinic, but this time I chose a different doctor. I had to settle for a male, but at least all my documents were already filed. My new doctor's name was Dr. Henry Frikker.

## Shakin' in My Boots

During one of my seizures, I felt like my circuit breaker was going bonkers. All the electrical currents seemed to be going haywire, like jolts of electricity zapping my brain. Neurons were misfiring and the damaged cells around the tumour were being punished with shock treatments. The truth is, during a seizure, electrical signals in the brain cause the release of chemicals called neurotransmitters.

Besides experiencing warmth throughout my body and wanting to strip down to my skivvies, I was fully aware during a seizure that this wasn't acceptable behaviour. I didn't lose consciousness or black out. I didn't even find that I stared or had a blank look on my face. I tended to cover my gimpy hand with my fully functional hand.

When people asked about the experience, I explained that I felt a sense of panic and had to sit down; if there was no place to sit, I just stopped what I was doing and stood still. I can't tell you how many seizures I've had, but they scare me every single time. You'd think I might get used to dealing with them and be able to shrug it off, but no, absolutely not.

One day, I was so upset that the tumour was causing me such grief, disrupting my day-to-day activities. I started feeling sorry for myself, not understanding why it had to be the whole right side of my body. I was right-handed and needed that side of my body to cooperate. I needed my right hand for shifting gears and my right leg for driving. It was a really off-day. I did everything in my power to fight for my right, but

I guess I was wrong. I thought I'd try to soak all my sorrows away and have a nice bubble bath in the Jacuzzi tub.

*Relax? Are you kidding me?*

After such a nerve-wracking day, I was worried I might electrocute myself in the tub. I had this strange visual of my hand slapping and twitching uncontrollably, creating waves, *brain waves*, in the tub. I decided to abort my plan and get out of the water. I reached to turn down the jet control, as the bubbles were bombarding me with suds. But my right hand was so weak that I didn't have the strength to turn it. Tears streamed down my face and I knew I had to cease the waterworks or the tub would overflow.

"Stupid, rotten, good for nothing pills," I grumbled. "They're just money down the drain."

I wiped my eyes and dried the rest of myself off. It was just one of those days when you wish you'd never gotten out of bed.

## You Must Have the Wrong Number

One day, I got a call from an unfamiliar number. The secretary to the Division of Neurosurgery told me over the phone that my neurologist had requested a consultation for further management of this lesion.

*Thump-thump.* My heartbeat sped up and I got a sinking feeling in my stomach. This head trauma was affecting other areas of my body as well. One problem seemed to create another. I felt discomfort, accompanied by chest pain, making me worry about an angina attack. My poor ticker was racing… a neurosurgeon? This didn't sound good. It didn't sound good at all.

## Sweating Bullets

The results were in. I was sweating bullets as I entered the hospital grounds. I sat in a neurosurgeon's waiting room; it doesn't get any more unnerving than that. My name was called and I waited some more, now closer to the issue at hand.

That day, I met Dr. Sumnerve (not his real name) for the first time. He pulled up the scans of my brain and I saw a white mass. I was still oblivious to the fact that this was an image of *my* brain. That had to be someone else's head…

I used to do my Arnold Schwarzenegger impersonation and say, "It's not a TUUMAR!"

*Tushay,* I told myself. *It is a tumour, and it's not funny anymore.*

"Your brain MRI was obtained and confirms the presence of a left cerebral hemispheric tumour." He spoke as nonchalantly as if ordering off a menu.

I took a big gulp. "A tumour?" Whenever I heard the word *tumour*, right away I associated it with the "C" word—cancer.

"The lesion is believed to be an epidermoid. It is benign, or not cancerous," he continued.

*Oh good. Finally, he's speaking English.* The rest of it was a bunch of neurosurgeon jargon. I stared at the computer screen, finally blinking when he reminded me of the presence of a definite abnormality. I remained dumbfounded, in a catatonic trance. I both did and didn't want to know more about this epidermoid, but I asked him anyway.

His exact words were, "Go home and Google it."

Unbelievable! The top dog, the highest MD on the rung of doctors, and not even *he* could give me a straight answer. I felt like a lost cause, a totally untreatable freak of nature.

## Talk to Me, Google

Hello, Google.

Epidermis cysts are typically benign congenital (present at birth) lesions. They represent nests of tissues misplaced during the embryonic life. They're smooth, with a glistening pearl-like sheen and may even have crystals in the centre. Usually, the epidermoid contains white, flaky debris. The word "debris," in my mind, meant garbage.

*Nice. My head's a landfill full of trash, a junk pile full of unwanted debris.*

I didn't know whether to continue reading or pick up the computer and smash it. The thought of having a compost heap in my head was revolting.

The article went on to say that an epidermoid is like a piece of jewellery, a pearl. Ironically enough, this gem in my noggin was my birthstone. Don't get me wrong, I would love to have a pearly white smile, but a whitish, fibrous, pearly tumour? No, not so much. I always thought it was a good thing to find a pearl in an oyster. But the world wasn't my oyster. Anyone feel like shucking oysters? Pass, I'm not in the mood. Anyone want to be the lucky recipient of a pearl necklace?

*Oh wait, Google has more…*

Epidermoids constitute approximately 0.2 to 1.8% of all brain tumours. Patients usually aren't symptomatic until between the ages of twenty to forty years because they're very slow growing and take a long time to expand to a problem-causing size. Basically, the cyst developed in my nervous system before I was even born. Let's put it this way: I may have been living with it my whole life, but I'm sure glad I hadn't known it was there.

Just when I came to terms with the tumour symbolizing a valuable pearl, I discovered it was a fluid-filled sac. Some contain a waxy substance while others are filled with a flaky material consisting of sweat glands, hair follicles, and dermal appendages. Some even resemble furuncles.

*What uncle is this now? Some long lost relative I wished I never knew existed!*

Let's face it. No matter how glorious I made this obstruction out to be, it would never be a pearl or a crystal. I couldn't disguise it. Mine sounded more like a furry moth with an ugly, bumpy thorax. The metamorphosis in the membrane had made a mistake and turned into a giant moth instead of a beautiful butterfly. Even if you add some bright and cheery colours to an insect, it's still an insect.

From what I gather, some skin cells became trapped in my nervous system as it was developing, thereby creating a repugnant deformity. I wished someone here on earth knew what to do about it.

## Queasy Does It

After looking at this information and imagining what the tumour was made of, I remembered having a weak stomach. So much so that it brought a story to mind. A few years back, I drove my mom to Regina. She was scheduled for day surgery on her right hand. She had Carpal tunnel syndrome. It was getting to the point that she was losing feeling in her hand, and sometimes she would even drop things. It could've been caused from excessive typing.

On our way back home, she started explaining the procedure and how she had been awake the whole time. The doctors had been carrying on a day-to-day conversation. Mom had been able to feel them working on her hand, but she had to look away.

She didn't get very far into the details. I was supposed to be her driver, but I had to resign. I felt myself becoming squeamish. I slammed on the brakes, practically swerving into the ditch, and parked the car all cockeyed on the shoulder. I jumped out of the car like the gas tank was on fire.

My head between my knees, I was sure I was going to upchuck. After I got enough fresh air, thought of something more pleasant, composed myself, and paced the ditch for a few minutes, I felt better.

My mother got out of the passenger seat, eyed her bandaged hand, and held out her left hand. "Here, give me the keys. I'll drive."

## Insomniac

To sleep, perchance to dream… not a chance! It takes me forever to fall asleep, unlike Alex, for whom it's lights out as soon as his head hits the pillow.

"Must be nice… instant ZZZs," I muttered to myself while counting sheep.

I lay tossing and turning, yawning yet not sleeping. I wasted so much time trying to fall asleep.

I wish I could shut my thinking cap off at night, but the sandman rarely visits me at a decent hour. Someone once told me to drink warm milk and I'd fall asleep like a baby. The only problem is that I've never drank a glass of milk in my life. I was allergic to milk when I was a baby; I had to drink Soyalac.

My mind goes round and round like a hamster wheel, going nowhere fast. The same thoughts repeat over and over. I have all day to think. I wish I could just shut my mind off and drift into Never Never Land. Instead I find that I turn nonstop, like a rotisserie. A lot of the time I watch the clock, which seems to laugh at me as insomnia takes its toll.

## In a Nutshell

I was always a little apprehensive about telling people about my brain tumour. On my list of top ten people to contact, however, was my friend Jody. She didn't think she heard me right, so I had to repeat my story. Her simple solution: "Why don't they just crack your head open like a walnut and take it out?" I actually laughed at her smart aleck remark.

It just wasn't that easy. Unfortunately, the tumour wasn't on the surface of my head. Oh no, nothing is simple in my world. It had to reside way down inside my skull. It sounded like the neurosurgeon would have to go through a canal, dig a ditch, trench in, and hope for the best. He didn't sound confident enough for my liking. He warned me that I could develop paralysis. He put it bluntly and told me I could end up in a wheelchair—should something go wrong (in other words, if he screwed up).

Alex and I had brand new hardwood floors that even a moccasin could scratch. A big chair with pimped-out wheels wasn't an option in our house. Dr. Sumnerve must be half-cracked to think I'd even consider it.

I went on to describe to Jody the indescribable: the attacks had happened countless times, yet I still couldn't put into words what had actually occurred. Jody sounded interested in the recurring power surge in my head.

"I want to see this thing in action!" she exclaimed.

"No comment."

Nope. She couldn't just let it go.

"You know, this little problematic, uh…complication of yours could come in handy if you ever play charades." She clapped her palms together, still deep in thought. "Ooh, ooh, I know. I've got a good one! Guess what it is."

My voice raised a pitch. "Oh, come off it!"

"Just bear with me."

"This is absurd," I groaned.

"Don't be such a killjoy. Now, here are your clues. It's a four-word phrase and it's also a song… okay, ready?" She started acting by taking a couple of first steps.

"Walking… simple," I mumbled, playing the party pooper.

She nodded. Next, she rolled her hands over one another, as if to say, "Go on."

I spurted out the first thing that came to my mind. "Walking on… sunshine."

Jody vigorously shook her head. Her bangs swung from side to side, sweeping across her forehead.

"Walkin' on broken glass," I shouted, figuring I'd hit the nail on the head.

My friend's face contorted into a look I'd never seen before. The thought of stepping on broken glass was enough to make her cringe. Jody wasn't the silent type and she couldn't stand it anymore. The whole button-your-lip-or-zip-it thing wasn't working for her. I knew I'd never get the silent treatment from the Jodester.

She caved. "Now, pretend your hand is like a traffic officer, directing—"

"Traffic," I cut her off in mid-sentence. "Play by the rules! If you're going to play charades, *play* charades. You can only act and nod; you're not allowed to talk. Don't be so daft!" And suddenly, I was all for the game and carrying on like a persnickety, snotty teenager. I started demonstrating what my hand did when it was having its temporary lapse. So, third word: Shaky.

"Yep, you got it!" She was thrilled, but knew all she could do was curl her lips under her teeth. Jody started sauntering around the room, pointing to the floor.

"Walking on shaky… floors? Umm… floor joists? By Jove, I think I've got it! Ground. Walking on shaky ground."

"*Aplauso!*" Jody clapped her hands together loudly, like she was acting out a commercial for a clap-on/clap-off light demo. "Man o' livin'! I figured you'd never get it."

"We're only having one frivolous round of this. Enough's enough. No more poking fun of me."

"Scout's honour," she promised, cocking her head to the side and batting her eyelashes.

"Pinky swear?" I asked, arching an eyebrow.

I heard an audible sigh. Because we were best buds, all was forgiven. At least we didn't have to worry about walking on eggshells. Not a funny *yolk*, I know. Boo me off the stage…

Angela Freriks

## Short Circuit

Jody wasn't the only one who wanted to see me short out. Dr. Neurotron asked if I could videotape the goings on. Me, myself, and my tumour all tried to make a video. The only trouble was that my hand didn't want to cooperate with the production. Many times I'd have to yell, "Cut!" I was trying to record the episode on my cell phone. The problem was, whenever I felt it coming on, I'd have to sit down. By the time I got to the couch and figured out the cell, the predator in my head decided to take five.

After several trial runs, I finally got some good footage. I only had about a ten-second warning before a seizure, so I had to act quickly… and *action!* I ran to the table, hopped up on the pub-style chair, flipped open the cell, and hit record. I somehow managed to hold it with my left hand and let the right hand run its course. This incident only lasted about thirty seconds—I think I got ten, give or take.

I had to hurry before my hand crapped out on me. "Gotcha," I cried out. Capturing the episode was tough, as though it had a criminal mind and was trying to outsmart me. The unwelcome tenant was taking up valuable cranial space and wasn't paying rent, and I was ready to post an eviction notice: "You *no* pay rent—you get *out!*"

I chuckled to myself and wondered if I should email my video to Wal-Mart and see if they'd hire me as a greeter.

After the filming of *Sporadic Seizures*, I knew I had exactly what the doctor had ordered. It definitely looked like an amateur home video. It looked like it was shot by the same videographer as *The Blair Witch Project*. But it wasn't the cameraman's fault; it was the faulty hand itself, shaking and causing all the distortion. Kill the lights…show's over!

On my next visit to Dr. Neurotron, I showed him the video of my hand flopping around like a fish on dry land.

"Oh, this is good!" he said, eyes lighting up. Now he could put a face to the symptoms.

My grandma, however, was bothered by my dysfunctional hand. While we were all gathered around the table one evening, I reached for some potatoes and froze mid-reach, drawing attention to myself. As I held my hand in front of my plate, it twitched and jumped as if I was conducting an orchestra.

Grandma looked away. "I don't like to see that."

It's all in the script, Gram. All in the script.

## Oh, My Aching Back
*December 2010*

I had a horrendous year. Right before Christmas, I felt like a turtle trying to walk on his hindquarters. I moved about as slow as a tortoise, too. My whole year seemed like it had been consumed with doctor appointments and prescription pickups. I couldn't believe I couldn't finish out the year without making an appointment with a chiropractor.

I walked into the clinic stooped over, looking like the Hunchback of Notre-Dame. Dr. Bycracky gave me a treatment, hoping to improve my posture. I was sent for X-rays which confirmed a slipped disk. Darn the luck.

The whole week was pretty much a write-off. I ended up going twice a day for chiro treatments and had to take a day off work. My stubbornness made me return to work the next day, though; my clients were counting on me to have their houses cleaned before Christmas. I figured I'd pretty much be hunched over vacuuming and scrubbing bathrooms anyway.

I had instructions from Dr. Bycracky to do my exercises and put ice on my back. I hated being cold, so I lay in front of the fireplace with a bag of peas. My last visit to the chiropractor was on December 22.

Two days later, Alex and I drove to Weyburn for Christmas Eve. When I opened a gift from one of my clients, I saw that it was a box of

Turtles. I opened the lid, took a peek, and found them all snug in their beds. *Their* backs looked fine. My client probably didn't anything of it, but I had a good laugh.

## Laughter Is the Best Medicine

I distinctly recall one of my favourite T-shirts as a happy-go-lucky kid. It had a clown on the front along with the words "Laugh, kid, laugh." Back then, I didn't have a care in the world.

After the diagnosis, I wasn't exactly a barrel of monkeys. Throughout the year, I regressed from human to Cro-Magnon to chimp. My moods had me swinging from sweet to sombre. One minute I was coping, but then, after a seizure, a storm hit. I'd become an angry ape. One day I was like a gorilla; I wanted to beat my hands against my chest and scream.

The seizures were taking control of my life and I'd gotten to the point where I didn't want to venture too far from home. I used my own discretion and quit some of my cleaning jobs. I had a couple clients on the west end of the city, but in order to get there I had to cross a bridge. Crossing the bridge in rush hour traffic caused me stress. I knew the seizures were random. If one were to strike on the bridge, I knew I'd have nowhere to pull over.

## Summary

2010 was the worst chapter of my life to that point. I felt like a half-dead mouse being batted around by a bunch of different alley cats (okay, fine… doctors). Being diagnosed with a brain tumour was a total shock to me and my family. Much of the year's conversation revolved around my medical handicap.

My debilitating situation disrupted my daily activities. I felt like such a Schleprock, carrying a heavy burden with dark rainclouds overhead. Some gloomy, dismal days, as streams turned into rivers of tears, I felt like hiring a rescue crew to pile sandbags to hold back floodwaters. Because when it rains, it pours. Unless you've had a brain tumour, you can't truly understand what someone goes through. The thing I learned the most that year was empathy.

Sayonara, 2010!

# part two

## Let's See What 2011 Has in Store…

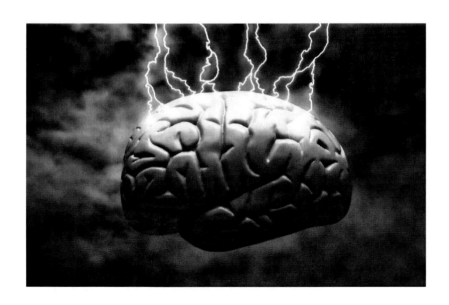

## Hey, Remember Me?

In the New Year, I went about living my life as normal. I actually managed to forget there was anything wrong with me, until he (the hunk trapped in my head) tapped me on the left side of my brain, and said, "I'm back. Miss me?" I had been seizure-free for twenty-five days, and then my head decided to unleash the beast.

Alex and I were at a drug store when it happened—go figure. I stopped in my tracks as I felt my face flush and my body get hot. Fear set in, as I'd always been scared I would have a full-blown epi-fit one day. I was worried I might fall on the floor, or just drop dead. I felt the need to hang onto something. Alex was nowhere in sight; he was in the magazine section, ogling muscle cars.

Anxiety gripped me, and in turn I gripped a flimsy cardboard display filled with bottles of vitamins. Naturally, I used my dominant hand to grasp the display, but I realized too late that it wasn't a wise move, as my dominant hand was the dud that didn't want to cooperate. When I started to shake, it was like an earthquake as the tower of vitamins trembled. I had to let go, praying that all the bottles didn't come crashing down, along with my world. I worried about falling. I imagined the commotion and embarrassment of a voice booming over the intercom, "Clean-up in aisle five, please. I repeat, assistance needed for vitamin spill."

After this, Alex and I went home. I never knew when my mind was going to play tricks on me—tumour tricks! This creature lurking about in my cranium made me feel like a schizo. Thank goodness the Mexican jumping bean in my cerebellum left the scene, and so did we. That was *loco!* Move on... nothing to see here.

When I got home, I was irate. If looks could kill...

"How dare you embarrass me like that in public!" I scolded the tumour. "You need to have a timeout. Go to your room and think about what you've done. I will not tolerate bad behaviour."

## Tumour Has It

"Word on the street is you have a brain tumour. Is that correct?" Amanda, one of my friends from Weyburn, asked me after she heard the tumour rumour. That was typical of a small city—word spreads like wildfire. Everyone knew everyone.

I decided to call Amanda to set the record straight. She was relieved to hear from me. "I've been so worried about you," she said. "I heard you have cancer."

"No. Lots of people misconstrue the word *tumour* and assume the worst."

"I've been checking the obituaries every day to make sure you're not in there." She sounded genuinely sick about my supposed death sentence.

I found it really disturbing to hear that my friend had thought I was either in palliative care or otherwise dying of cancer, if not dead already. Checking the obits... how morbid!

## Let's Give 'Em Something to Blog About

Extra! Extra! Read all about it. People thrive on news. Bad news, especially. Bad weather and poor health are probably the top two on the list. People relish gossip and feed off others' tribulations. If I were a celebrity, I would've been in the tabloids.

Not much can trump a brain tumour. The headlines would have read: "Self-employed maid demoted to unemployed maid… diagnosed with brain tumour." Anyone down on their luck could say, "I guess my life doesn't seem so bad now."

Before you stick your foot in your mouth and flap your lips about someone else, though, do a shoulder check. Turn around and make sure the person isn't sitting in the booth directly behind you. When you say something bad about another, realize that it's considered slander. It's never good to gossip. If you don't have anything good to say, don't say it all.

## 39 and Holding

On my last night of being thirty-eight, I lay in bed and watched the digital clock turn past midnight. *Yes! I made it to thirty-nine. Now I can go to sleep and get some shuteye before celebrating my big day.*

My alarm clock woke me up to a good song on the radio. I was too groggy to care, so I reached over and slapped the slumber bar. It was getting to be after 8:00 a.m. No more snoozes.

"Jumpin' Gemini!" I said to myself, looking in the bathroom mirror. I scrunched up my nose. *Are you serious? A zit, at my age?* Whenever I get a zit, I call it Dot, short for Dorothy. *She* was staring me right in the face, so I blotted Dot with concealer and clicked off the light.

As a creature of habit, I next awaited a cup of freshly brewed coffee. I had the same old, same old for breakfast everyday: a chocolate chip banana bran muffin. Along with this carbohydrate of choice, I grabbed a chrome travel mug and headed out the door.

My husband arrived home from work early. He wished me a happy birthday as we went to the hospital. By now it was standard procedure: we wandered over to the admitting station and waited for my name to be called. As I took a seat at unit one, the lady behind the desk asked, "What day is your birthday?"

My answer was a mellow, unenthusiastic, "Today."

"Oh." She looked back down at my health card. "Well, you'll have to go out and party it up tonight."

"Not."

We took our seats in yet another room and waited… and waited. While waiting, I took note of my surroundings. The two ladies at the front desk were laughing and joking around. Everyone else had the same sombre look. I didn't take the time to count heads; I only took notice of the interesting ones. One lady had her nose in a book. Boring. Another man, in a wheelchair, was hacking and excreting phlegm. I thought he might cough up a lung, or need a pail. I had to look away, fearing that my face showed an expression of utter disgust. A gentleman to my left was wearing socks and sandals. This is a *fashion faux pas* in my books. His socks were gray, but I noticed the black heel patch on the top of his foot.

*You'd think it would be a natural thing to flip that sucker over and put it on the proper way,* I thought. I guess an uncomfortable sock was the least of this man's concerns. After all, he was in the hospital waiting for a neurosurgical consultation.

What I saw next made me blink. I did a double-take, my fingers drumming against my chin, and said, "Suspicious." I watched two policemen escorting, wait for it… a prisoner. This convict didn't stand out; he wore everyday attire instead of black-and-white vertical stripes or a classic pumpkin orange jumpsuit.

The thing that caught my attention was that he, like all the others, including myself, had the same solemn look on his face, and rightfully so. I couldn't help but feel for him. He didn't sit with us in the waiting room. Later, coming out of a back room, the man shuffled his feet, rattling his leg chains. He wore handcuffs as he was escorted into the doctor's office. The officers accompanied the man during his visit.

As I sat in my cold vinyl chair, I thought about how unfair life is. The prisoner got to have a somewhat normal day and wear actual street clothes. Our city catchphrase is "Saskatoon Shines!" Well, he got to be out in the sunlight, in the heart of Saskatoon, but he only caught a brief glimpse of the real world. He went from one institute to another. I bowed my head and let out a sigh.

Soon, Dr. Sumnerve came into the waiting room, grabbed my chart, and called us in. My heart was pounding a little harder than usual. I felt like I should be the one with chains around my ankles; I was ready to run or do whatever it took to get me out of there. No doubt like that prisoner, I wanted my life back. No, this should be in all caps—I WANTED MY LIFE BACK!

I felt like my life had been completely stripped away from me. I was living in my own prison, in lockdown, with the imposter in my head. The tumour was trapped in a cell—*a brain cell.*

*Okay, Ang, get it together. Listen to what the doc has to say.*

I had pushed for this appointment, but now that the time had come, I sat there discombobulated. For my birthday, I hadn't asked for a new car with all the bells and whistles; I just wished to be out of this predicament.

## Ixnay on the Bi-op-say

The most important thing Dr. Sumnerve had to say was that "we" had to try to control the seizures.

"I'll see you again in about a month's time for a follow up," he said. "We'll see if doubling the dose helps. Then we'll discuss if we should do a biopsy to determine what type of tissue it is."

Out of the blue, he went on to explain that for the biopsy he'd have to shave some hair and use a big needle to extract a tissue sample.

"Now, this *is* surgery… so you *will* have to stay in the hospital for a couple of days," he explained. "You may be off work for a couple of weeks as well. We have to make an incision about yeh big." He estimated the size with his thumb and forefinger.

*Are you kidding me right now?* I asked myself.

I sank into a catatonic trance. The whole conversation made me ill. I knew full-well that no one was going to insert an enormous cow needle into my head! My brain was frightened about the syringe size guesstimate. The tumour wanted to shrink down and hide, terrified of being poked, probed, and prodded.

I had no further questions. I was *so* done listening to all this neurosurgeon gobbledygook. I made a decision right then and there that unless I got worse—way, *way* worse—no one would go poking around in my head. I hoped there would be an easy answer to my "head case," but the trial continued; I was scheduled for another MRI in September. The doctor wanted to monitor this rare form of some unbeknownst-to-me thing every three months.

The doctors involved wanted to know if I could figure out what triggered the seizures. Alex and I had recently started jogging, but every time I ran I had a seizure. Alex mentioned this to Dr. Sumnerve and he shrieked, his diatonic scale ascending a couple octaves. "No running," he warned us. "Just take brisk walks. This is a fragile time!"

The ticket for parking cost me an arm and a leg, so fortunately we were only there for a short time. Still wearing the same face, I commented to Alex that it would have been cheaper to take a limo. I tend to exaggerate a bit, but this was robbery… there's nothing like kicking a guy when he's down.

## Make a Wish, Birthday Girl!

Now that I'd gotten my appointment over with, I hoped to enjoy the rest of my day. I got home, took a pair of scissors, and snipped the hospital bling off my right wrist. The same day, thirty-nine years earlier, I had been born in the hospital, wearing my very first ID bracelet.

My mom called to wish me, her one and only child, a happy birthday. I told her how I had stayed awake to bid thirty-eight adieu; I had wanted to make sure I lived to be thirty-nine… God willing.

She laughed and told me about how my grandpa had told her the exact same story. Apparently he had also lain awake on the night prior to his birthdays to make sure he could say he had lived to be a certain age. The only difference was that my grandpa was in his nineties at the time!

Yeah, I guess that's pretty bad. Only in my thirties and I was already starting to worry about getting old, even though I had nearly sixty years to go if I was going to catch up to Grandpa. He'd lived to be the ripe, or shall I say *pruney*, old age of ninety-seven.

Alex asked me what I wanted for my birthday and I simply replied, "A new head." Instead he offered to take me to dinner and a movie. *Soul Surfer* was playing, a movie I thoroughly enjoyed, and I couldn't have watched it on a better day. I was feeling kind of discouraged and the movie lifted my spirits. No matter how hard life can be, God will give us the strength to pull through.

I could empathize with the main character in the movie, Bethany Hamilton. She'd lost her arm to a shark while surfing, her passion in life. At the beginning of the movie, she got discouraged and couldn't understand why this had happened to her. I, too, have questioned God's reasoning.

Some of my favourite activities are walking, biking, and jogging—and I had just been informed that I should refrain from jogging. It was heart-wrenching to have something I enjoyed so much be stripped away from me. I hoped that one day I'd be able to pick up the pace and start jogging again. My new goal was to return to running, but this time for a different purpose. At the end of the run, I wanted to be able to spit out these words: "I got my life back!"

If I had to serve a life sentence with this brain tumour, I prayed it wouldn't give me too much grief. If I had to be on medication or monitor the tumour by going for MRIs for the rest of my life and deal with weirdness in my face, so be it.

We have to take each day as it comes. If life kicks us when we're down, we just have to get back up on our feet and continue fighting.

## Make a Mountain out of a Molehill

Two days after my birthday, I felt a nudge. Something was telling me to challenge myself. The neurosurgeon had suggested that I not run, as it could trigger a seizure. So, I determined to do something highly not recommended.

Everyone knows that Saskatchewan is flat. Born and raised on the prairies, my legs are used to functioning on low ground with little to no incline. I'm not a competitive person by nature, but I am stubborn. I felt like I needed to face my uphill battle, and what better way was there to meet the challenge head-on except to climb the face of Grouse Mountain?

My cousin Laurie and I had done the Grouse Grind back in 2004 on a trip to Vancouver. A few years can make a big difference. Back then I was in much better shape—I ran, went to the gym, faithfully did sit-ups every morning, and I even joined a co-ed soccer team.

I don't know what it is about the sudden desire to conquer a task. I was determined to succeed on this mission—a mountain mission. I felt inspired to encourage others to conquer their dreams. After being diagnosed with a brain tumour, I needed to experience a strong sense of accomplishment. I had gumption, and Grouse was calling my name.

When I asked Dr. Sumnerve what he thought about me climbing a mountain, he skirted the question like a politician. I think it took a minute for my question to register. One minute I was desperately seeking an answer to my seizure disorder, and the next I wanted to put my life in jeopardy. I got the impression he thought I was Looney Tunes.

"It's your prerogative," he said, his voice lowering a notch.

He didn't outright give me permission; he wouldn't want to take a chance on feeling guilty in case I took a spill. He told me he'd heard cases of people wanting to accomplish something extreme after a diagnosis. I got the impression he frowned upon the idea of overexertion, but I knew climbing a mere hill (or in Saskatchewan, a speed bump) was hardly worth it. There was no challenge in that. That's why I decided to trek up a *real* mountain.

My mind was made up to get back into shape. I decided to give myself a couple months of training. Along with my sidekick Alex, I agreed to start walking, biking, and climbing.

Grouse Mountain, in British Columbia, is also known as "Mother Nature's stair master." The climb is rated difficult. It's a rugged terrain of 2,830 steep steps—3,700 feet to the top! This is more than a twelve-step program. The average time needed to complete the hike is an hour and a half. To be on the safe side, we set aside two.

Seizures may slow some patients down, but not me. If the infuriating mass presented itself, I would let it run its course and carry on. If I had six seizures as I headed up the mountain, I'd say, "Bring it on." I would stop and rest, but carry on. I would persevere and pursue my dream until I reached the top!

## Knowledge on Board

Alex and I decided to attend a brain tumour support group. It was held once a month at Royal University Hospital. But when we got to the meeting room, I didn't see a tumour in sight. We paced the hall until we heard a ding as the elevator reached the fourth floor. A man asked if we were here for the support group.

He hadn't expected anyone to show up because the meetings had wrapped up for the season. We hadn't realized the meetings weren't held during the summer holidays. However, he did take the time to introduce himself. We sat down and exchanged stories. He then explained about what took place at the support group.

He invited Alex and me to his home, as he had forgotten the information pamphlets by his front door. We went over to his house and met his wife. They invited us in for coffee and I perused the pamphlets. I borrowed some books, CDs, and DVDs to help me learn more about brain tumours.

## Work It, Girl

It was now getting towards the end of June. In approximately two months, I would tackle Grouse. I had training to do. Alex and I decided the best place in Saskatoon to put our legs to the test was the seventy-nine steps to the top of the CP Railway Bridge. It provided a beautiful view of the river as well.

On the day we went, it was raining slightly. I tried to think of it as a light mist. I hoped the stairs weren't slippery because I would hate to slip and fall on my first day of setting out to get my limbs in shape.

I had no idea how this was going to go. I told Alex that for our first attempt, we should shoot for ten—ten sets of seventy-nine stairs. I was afraid I'd be huffing and puffing like The Little Engine That Could, saying, "I think I can, I think I can."

The first step, they say, is to admit you have a problem. So I did. I admitted it: "I'm Angela, and I have a brain tumour."

After the tenth ascent of those grated stairs, crossing the bridge, then climbing down another flight of wooden steps, we crossed the street. We decided to walk to the car, chug back some water, and assess how we felt. Surprised at myself, I felt good.

"Maybe I shouldn't push myself too hard the first day," I suggested to Alex.

## Cranium Crisis

I wondered what part of my body didn't like this the most—my legs, the tumour, my ticker, or my neck. I was afraid my neck would get sore as I had to keep my head down with my eyes focused on the stairs. Anyone who has climbed those grated stairs knows that it can give you a trippy feeling. It's like your eyes play tricks on you. The first two flights of stairs seemed normal, but when I looked down through the holes in the grate and saw the stairs *under* the stairs, I wondered if this was the same effect as taking some kind of weird drug. I decided it was in my best interest to guide myself up using the handrails. I knew the mountain wasn't going to give me a railing, so maybe I'd end up on all fours, grasping for rocks embedded in the mountainside.

We decided to tackle a few more climbs. On our descent, I saw a lady who was also climbing several times.

"Are we having fun yet?" I asked her.

I don't recollect getting a direct answer. It was more like, "I better keep moving before it starts to pour."

We went up those steps a total of nineteen times. That's 1,501 stairs! That was halfway up Grouse. Awesome! I was proud of myself and my tumour left me alone during my workout. I felt encouraged and hoped to continue my training.

I had a bad feeling, though, that our legs might feel like jello the next day. Jello sounded like a great idea, so I went ahead and made some, adding a can of mandarin oranges. (I remembered from my running days that gelatin was recommended.) We slurped it down.

The next day, I was concerned about my stilts being in agony, but only our calves were tender. I wasn't being a pessimist... just a realist, figuring my legs would be all jiggly, wobbly, and rubbery. I'm grateful to Alex for being my motivator. It takes two to tango.

Angela Freriks

# Lynn Valley (North Vancouver)
*August 23, 2011*

Alex, Dad, and I decided to go to Lynn Valley Canyon. It wasn't Mom's forte to be adventurous. First things first—I did a little stretching as I prepared for the hiking trails. I'm not entirely sure if this was the smartest thing to do or not, as this was pre-climb day, but time was of the essence. We only had four days in Vancouver, so we needed to get our priorities straight. We all wanted to see Lynn Valley and, believe it or not, it wasn't raining in Vancouver... so, off we went.

When we stepped onto the Lynn Canyon suspension bridge, it started swaying. Alex had never been on a swinging bridge before, but when he got halfway across he looked below and was mesmerized by the view. My dad had a fear of heights. When he looked down, he made a ghostly sound. We were really high up and if the bridge had chosen that moment to give out, we would have been goners.

"Gives me the willies," Dad said as he shuddered and headed for steady ground.

We made it across the bridge safe and sound. The scenery was beautiful and we started our hike down the trail. After hiking and climbing a few wooden stairs, we stumbled upon a waterfall. We looked up and saw a few crazy teenagers who had climbed to the top and were about to jump off a ledge.

"Jumpers!" I called out. I hoped these insane punks didn't have suicidal tendencies. After one had the guts to freefall, the others felt compelled to follow. One girl jumped and screamed all the way down until she landed in the water. It was something to witness. I was the one with the brain tumour, but I had more common sense than that. When she surfaced, it was like she was in shock. Her body shook and her teeth chattered. She perched herself up on a monstrous rock as her friend handed her a towel. The sopping wet daredevil was freezing to death and could have had a coronary; she was babbling and dropping F-bombs.

"I chee wah wah! The girl's got quite a mouth on her," I exclaimed, my eyes and mouth wide open.

"I'd say." Alex was appalled at her profanity. "I'm sure her mother would frown upon hearing her daughter's potty mouth."

Another thrill seeker was ready to perform her fear factor stunt. After her friend's experience, we could sense the girl was apprehensive, but she knew she had to take one for the team. She climbed up the side of the cliff on all fours, like a mountain goat. She dug her hooves into the rocks and clawed her way up. She, too, hollered all the way down. When she bobbed up, her bikini top fell down and she quickly fumbled around to adjust it. When I saw it was becoming like a Vegas night show, I leaned over and covered Alex's eyes. The little mermaid had given everyone a free peep show. She swam so fast I thought a shark was after her. She flopped onto the rock and I thought the nimrod was going to suffer from hypothermia. I'm not sure what the temperature of the water was, but unless you happened to be a polar bear, I couldn't understand the attraction.

We left the unexpected scene of buoyant boobies and carried on along nature's path. I wanted to make sure I didn't wear out my legs for tomorrow's big event.

The trail spit us out at a quaint little coffee shop. We sat down and had a snack and a cup of joe. It felt good to sit. We needed to regain our energy.

## Note to Self: Must Walk Seawall

Vancouver is one of Canada's most beautiful cities. While we were on the west coast, I figured we should walk along the seawall. It was populated with joggers, bicyclists, and rollerbladers. People these days are great at multi-tasking; the majority of the human race was talking or texting on their mobile devices. I can only seem to use one side of my brain at a time, and the left side was obstructed! I thought I was doing well just by walking and talking at the same time, not to mention sightseeing.

I was enjoying the ocean breeze, listening to the waves of the Pacific dance against the seawall. Alex and I walked along the beach and put our toes in the sand. We then took a stroll to a dock where we noticed seals all lined up against one another.

Our heads were tilted skyward as we appraised the high-rise buildings and tried to decide how much they were worth. Gazing up, I cooed dreamily, "Imagine the view from the top of a skyrise… I'll have me one of those penthouse suites, when I make my first million."

"Pipe dreams, my love," said Alex.

It was getting to be dusk and we could see the city lights reflecting off the ocean. The Lion's Gate Bridge was lit up and we were only a few footprints in the sand away. We watched the sea bus as it crossed over to Vancouver.

I knew the next body of water we would see was the South Saskatchewan River, right in Saskatoon.

## Wife and Spouse Climb Grouse
### *August 24, 2011*

There we were on August 24 at approximately 9:30 in the morning, ready to commence our spiralling journey to the peak of Grouse Mountain. I stood beside a big yellow sign with all the caution rules. I ignored them. I stretched my legs and tried to limber up before taking many vigorous steps up the mountain. Our support group, party of two (Ma and Pa), were there to cheer us on. Those wussies took the skyride up.

Alex wore a camera around his neck and videotaped the journey up. The first few steps were a breeze. We found out soon enough, though, that it was a challenge. We both exerted ourselves, panting like we'd been sitting in a sauna for way too long. We decided to find somewhere along the way to park our heinies. As we rested, I grabbed the water out of the backpack and slurped it down, making annoying gulping sounds. We then hoisted ourselves up and carried on with beads of sweat dripping down our faces.

Every now and then, Alex cranked his neck around and bellowed, "How ya doing back there?"

"Keep going," I reported back. "It's not like we're trying to conquer Mount Kilimanjaro."

Around the three-quarter mark, an aura warned me of a seizure coming on. I let one guy pass me as I let my body do its thing. I had my doubts whether it would leave me alone long enough for me to make it to the top. However, I continued on and we completed our mission, reaching the summit in an hour and thirty-two minutes. Hurray! Alex was at the summit waiting for me and he had the camera rolling. I declared that I had a tumour, reached in my backpack, and held up a Brain Tumour Imagine a Cure magnet.

Brain tumours are more common than people think. It's estimated that more than 55,000 people in Canada live with a brain tumour and more than 10,000 people are newly diagnosed each year. For whatever reason, I was cursed with one, but I wasn't going to let it ruin my life.

## High Hopes

My world changed when I found out about the tumour. Because my struggle hit so close to home, I wanted to make a difference in other peoples' lives, so I decided to raise money. The funds my family and I collected before the Grouse Mountain climb would help bring the Brain Tumour Foundation of Canada closer to their goal of finding a cure and raising awareness. Proceeds were for research.

I'd like to mention a special thank you to my parents, who collected pledges, and to the many others who donated generous amounts.

Angela Freriks

# Companion and Compassion from Above

I've always thought of myself as a follower of Jesus. He's been my closest friend and has been with me every step of the way. The one thing I don't understand is why bad things happen to good people. Some people have said things to me like, "Maybe this is happening for a reason" or "The tumour is not from God." I wanted to scream and ask, "Then what's the reason?" I know it's not from God. God doesn't plant evil things in our minds; therefore, I wanted it out of my head.

The word of God (the Bible) is sharper than any double-edged sword. When my life presented me with this wake-up call, I went straight to the source, looking for encouraging words from God. Mom received an email from one of her friends who recommended reading from the Psalms.

## He Is My Shepherd

I've never considered myself a "lost sheep," but I've pleaded *sheepishly* with God to give me a second chance. I felt like a sheep that had gone astray for awhile. Perhaps I needed this scare tactic from God to smarten me up and show me how I needed to be closer to Him and get to know Him more.

If it wasn't through the comfort of Jesus and the peaceful image of Him holding me as a lamb of His flock, I don't think I could have pulled through this stressful situation on my own.

Throughout this trying time, I pictured myself like a lamb of God and felt comfort as He embraced me. I know I'm safe in His arms. I'm one of His flock and He calls me by name… Angela.

## Allll De Way to the Top

I once had a dream about seeing the pearly gates, and I often think about it. All I remember is that I was alone in an elevator. I pushed the up button and was on my way to heaven. As I reached the top, or shall I say the Kingdom, the doors opened and in the distance I saw the golden gates. I shot up in bed, happy to wake up alive, knowing that I wasn't ready for heaven... yet.

I know my name is written in His book and someday I'll enter His gates, but I realized I needed to practice songs so I would know the words when I got to heaven. I didn't want to be in heaven and have to look for a teleprompter. I wanted to refresh my memory on the obvious stories of Noah and the ark, Daniel in the lion's den, the whale that swallowed Jonah, and David and Goliath. I knew all these stories from my childhood; my parents had read them to me from a hardcover book with pictures.

## Cranial Cramp

Denying the necessity of surgery, I tried anything and everything I could think of to shrink the tumour, except acupuncture. I hunted for an answer to my unsolved mystery. It felt like I met with every kind of doctor. I was at my wit's end, lost in a house of mirrors, not knowing where to turn, and unable to find my way out.

I went to health food stores and inquired about herbal remedies, figuring I'd take a stab at alternative medication. While I was in the store, this nasty lump in my lobe decided to put on a show. Right in the middle of having a conversation with one of the girls who worked there, she stopped mid-sentence, furrowed her brow, and asked, "Are you alright?"

The next thing I knew, she was calling for her co-worker to get me a chair. This lady would have made an excellent first responder, as she rolled in a chair from the back within seconds. As I sat down, the first girl commanded the other one to get me some water and an Acai berry chewy vitamin, for energy. The two of them stood in front of me, bewildered, as if someone had called a code blue over the intercom—"Get that water over here, stat!"

After my hand quit shaking, I handed her the cup and got up like nothing had happened.

"You turned white as a ghost!" the girl exclaimed in a freaked-out tone.

"I'm good now. The stupid thing always does this to me at the most inopportune times," I remarked. Then I used a whisper-tone: "Shame on you, bad tumour!"

I'm happy to say there was no one else in the store at the time.

## Exhausting All My Options

One of the girls at the health food store recommended an immune-enhancing medicinal mushroom therapy. I called one of the distributers about the immune boosting mushrooms, which came in capsules. These "magic mushrooms" were supposed to give the body seven times the usual immune support. After talking to a few reps on the phone, one of them suggested I take two capsules, two hours apart.

I wanted to speak to the company's dealer to get his take on these healing shrooms. He could have easily sold me on this product, had he told me it would help, bragging up these fungus-filled antioxidants. It turned out he was completely honest and told me not to waste my money because it probably wouldn't work.

Another alternative treatment involved becoming a teetotaller. I'm well aware that Brits love their tea, but even a British bloke would decline the opportunity to wet his whistle with a cup of Essiac tea. I was warned that it tasted terrible—but it worked. The problem was I couldn't *do* bad tastes; the method of plugging my nose to swallow something distasteful just didn't work for me. I wasn't sure if I wanted to sip some potent potion and activate my gag reflexes. This just wasn't my cup of tea.

I also did research on the Mayo Clinic in Rochester, Minnesota and came to the conclusion that if it was costly, yet effective, then so be it.

After all, this was my *life*. You can't put a price on your health. If I had to travel outside the country… well, I would do whatever it took.

## Cut to the Chase

I took the initiative to contact the Gamma Clinic in Winnipeg. I'd read about and looked at pictures of the Gamma knife. This intrigued me. One guy referred to it as a "Star Trekky" procedure. It sounded like an out-of-this-world experience and much less invasive than actual *brain surgery*. I was game to go this route to get rid of the goober.

I was excited about this option, so I got on the horn and spoke with a friendly nurse who I liked from the get-go. She used terms of endearment. She was more than pleased to inform me that a biopsy wouldn't be required, but she did mention that a tumour could only be up to a certain size for the treatment to work.

She guided me with further instructions, explaining that my neurosurgeon would have to send a consult letter, along with the MRI scans. She said I could just call the surgeon's office and have them fax it. The doctor in Winnipeg would then decide whether this piece of *cutlery* could be used on me.

I thought I'd solved my own case when I talked to Dr. Sumnerve, but he basically told me the Gamma knife wasn't going to cut it. The tumour was too large.

Shot down! My bottom lip just about hit the floor when I was told I wasn't a suitable candidate.

Next, my thoughts turned to steroids. Steroids would shrink it. I smiled and thought, *I'm down with that!* I was told that by taking a few pills, the cranial clump could shrivel right up and disintegrate…vanish. Unfortunately, I found out that my kind of tumour wouldn't respond to this type of treatment.

Someone else told me about a treatment called OK 432 (an injection to shrink tumours, such as lymphangioma). This treatment was well-known in Europe. I wasn't sure what was worse, an injection or a resection. The idea of an injection into the tumour didn't appeal to me. But an actual resection or removal would be more invasive and sounded much worse. I decided to pass and keep searching.

## Urgent Email

Prior to finding out about the tumour, I emailed *The Doctors*, a TV show. I plunked in my whole spiel about my health concerns and asked if they had any suggestions. I was optimistic. Maybe it was something minor, like me being low in iron. Perhaps it could be because I consumed too much aspartame (from diet sodas).

Quite a bit of time passed without me receiving a reply. I felt rejected. I persevered and typed up a second email. This time, I spelled **Brain Tumour** in bold. In the email, I questioned if it could be Lyme disease, or Bell's Palsy.

I anticipated a response. I thought they might state the obvious and suggest I get a CT scan. Maybe one of the doctors could've asked, "Do you have the number for Johns Hopkins Hospital?" To which I would've replied, "No, go fish."

Next to the email was a little box that asked whether I would be willing to be a guest on the show. I checked it. I guess it was a rhetorical question because I got my answer: it's a no-go and a no-show. Obviously, no one wanted to touch this with a ten-foot poll, so I dropped it.

## Alternative Treatments

A few years back, I went to visit someone I would call a *quack*. She basically told me my fortune. Instead of looking into a crystal ball, she pushed on different areas of my feet. Never once did she bother to mention anything about me having a brain tumour. I went to see her because I had a sore back. Well, let's just say I never went back.

I was still completely stumped as to how to deal with the issue at hand. I then read an article in the paper about a new high-tech robotic arm: "Ah, *oui oui*! I shall go to Quebec!" I said in my best French accent, talking with my arms. Unfortunately, I couldn't fathom having a medical procedure done to my brain.

I read how the surgeon mapped out the area, having your MRI image on a screen while the robotic arm performed the procedure. To err is human; the human hand gets tired and tends to shake after a while, depending on the number of hours it takes to perform the surgery. One wrong move could be devastating or end your life. I needed extreme precision.

I was warned that because my tumour was so large, if something should happen during surgery, it could affect my right arm, cause weakness in my right leg, and result in my needing physio (worst case scenario, I could end up in a wheelchair). My speech could also be affected. I didn't want to take the risk.

I called a few naturopathic doctors after that, telling them my story. Not one of them was interested in tumour talk. One of them admitted she didn't even want to attempt it. I felt like a lost cause.

## Simple Solution

That is, until I called a homeopathic doctor by the name of Dr. Mandarin. While I was on the phone with him, I struggled to comprehend his strong accent.

"So, you've heard of an epidermoid cyst?" I asked.

"You come see me *dis* week," said the man with a hopeful remedy.

As I entered the waiting room, I saw a small child with an enormous growth on her cheek. At first I figured she had a jaw breaker in her mouth, but then I diagnosed it as a sebaceous cyst. I felt so sorry for her because it was clearly visible. At least no one knew about my tumour but me. To this day, I wonder whether or not Dr. Mandarin had an answer for that child.

I sat down and he inquired about my history as a child. He came up with a mixture of herbal concoctions and also told me the skin tag on my neck would fall off. I thought, *Where will it go?* I had a second skin tag under my arm, but I decided to monitor this one on my own. Maybe this statement was to prove to me that the physical evidence of my skin blemish would disappear. This, in turn, would make me believe he had the solution to my dilemma. He said that if I added four drops of this amazing cure-all to a bottle of water and sipped it all day long, my cyst would shrink.

Every morning, as part of my daily routine, I counted the drops into a bottle of water. I called it my "sippy sippy" drink. After a few weeks, I phoned him back and told him my MRI results showed there had been no change; I still had a big fat tumour in my head.

I went back to his office for a second time. He added one more ingredient to the other four. Surely now, by adding five pumps of this homeopathic medicine, costing over sixty dollars per bottle, I would see results. I was willing to give it one more chance; anything so I didn't have to go through brain surgery, right?

I remember thinking, *This stuff will either cure me or kill me.*

## Vamoose!

As of late, I found myself feeling paranoid about any little blip in my system. I kept looking in the mirror, but the blasted skin tag was still there and it hadn't gotten any smaller. Finally, I made a doctor's appointment to get these things taken care of. The doctor suggested using liquid nitrogen for the skin tags, which is a blast of freezing at ridiculously low temperatures. After one shot of this to my neck, I pictured myself like a cartoon skeleton being hit by a lightning bolt. Talk about a pain in the neck!

Suddenly, a freezing blast of intolerable pain shot under my arm and I wanted to scream at the top of my lungs. I received two treatments in one sitting and *ay-yi-yi,* did that hurt! Needless to say, it was all for nothing; the "freeze off" procedure (cryotherapy) didn't work.

While I was at the doctor's office, I complained of having numbness on the left side of my face; I described it as the same feeling as when Novocain wears off. He asked me if I was taking anything else he should know about. I told him about the homeopathic medicine and that the seizures were still happening. I'm pretty sure medical doctors don't agree with all this alternative stuff; if it's not in their medical books, they don't know what it is. He advised me to stop taking it… so I did. I quit cold turkey. No more partaking of the sippy sippy.

## Malfunction at the Junction

I was in the downtown core of Saskatoon when this confounded thing put a damper on my mood, literally crippling me with fear. From a physics aspect, the rate of the tumour's acceleration created a brain surge. I'd never actually tried walking on my gimpy leg before, and when I did, I found out in a hurry that it was dysfunctional. I was physically unable to walk and lost the mobility in my right leg. I didn't know whether to drag it behind me and look like an accident victim, or just limp a little and hope I didn't collapse. My equilibrium was so off that I stumbled around like I was drunk as a skunk. I did my best not to draw attention to myself, but I was worried someone might think I'd been tipping back a few wobbly pops. I'm not aware if anyone saw this incident go down; I don't recall any suspicious glares. Matter of fact, I stood there like a big bag of stupid!

## Have You Lost Your Marbles?

After suffering with this dirty rotter in my head, I got fed up. I wished I had a screw loose in my head to easily access and disassemble my cranium. I was tempted to run to the garage and get a screwdriver to fix my problem. (Righty tighty, lefty loosey)

The heck with it! My mind was giving me crazy ideas to get up in there, even using an exacto knife, to carve the sucker out myself. I'd wait until I felt a seizure coming on, then allow my symptoms to let me know where to go in and start extracting. Exacto mondo!

I envisioned playing the role of a mad scientist working on an experiment. Due to passing science class by the skin of my teeth, I refrained from pursuing this hair-brained idea. There was a method to my madness, but this wasn't the answer people meant when they told me to "keep an open mind."

## The Green Mile

One evening, *The Green Mile* was on TV. My husband and I decided to watch this movie marathon; with the commercials, I believe it was about four hours. Little did I know that the warden's wife had been diagnosed with an inoperable brain tumour! One of the prisoners on death row was known to have supernatural healing powers. His name was John Coffey. When the prison guards took John to the warden's house, John cured the man's wife; the tumour left her body.

My husband commented that he wished John Coffey was here to make my tumour go away. I know that no man can heal another man. A miracle happens through the healing hand of God. God alone deserves all the credit, glory, praise, and thanks. I believe that through faith, and only if it is God's will, you are healed.

## Stop, Drop, and Pray

There was nothing I, or anyone else, could do for me, so I gave all my burdens to the Lord and left them there. I prayed over and over that He would become my personal physician and make the seizures stop. I knew He was the Greatest Physician of all.

I felt like I should make a 911 call to God: "God, I have an emergency.

I need you to respond, and if not today, soon and *very* soon." It seemed like I prayed all day, everyday. I talked God's ear off. I rambled on for so long that I'm sure He felt like hanging up on me.

If it was just God and me, one on one, I could pray all day long! I'm sure He was saying, "Yes, I heard you the first time, my child. You don't need to say the same prayers repeatedly." I was starting to think God might be concerned that I had OCD. It's a good thing He's a patient God; I didn't mean to seem needy, but I really was.

I'm not one who likes any public show of affection. I've never prayed out loud. I remember squirming in my desk at school when it came time to do oral reading in front of the class.

Mom told me how she always drove by the Catholic Church and read new messages on the sign. One particular day, the sign read: "Make prayer your first choice, not your last resort."

Many people think there's nothing they need to request from God if life is sailing along smoothly. But when storms come their way, their hands are instantly clasped in prayer, pleading for God to solve their problem. Most people don't think to thank God for the things He has already done.

## Growing Concern
*September 12, 2011*

The time had come for another MRI. This time, there would be no pediatric needle. Request denied. A larger adult needle was used to inject the contrast media. This was to see what was going on inside my head. Afterward, I settled in to wait for news.

I had a neurologist appointment scheduled for September. Next to the calendar sticker of my doctor's appointment, I noticed there was going to be a full moon that night. Full moons are said to make people act weird, and here I was, on the verge of going crazy, living with this compost heap in my brain.

I complained to Dr. Neurotron about my seizures every month for a year and a half. He asked if I'd been keeping a journal. Each day I had a seizure, I circled the day in my calendar using red and marked down the number of times. One day I had a total of six seizures. I complained to him about them waking me up during the night. I told him that they were getting so bad that I finally gave up keeping track.

After doubling up on the dosage and still not improving, guess what? "Increase it more!" was his professional advice.

Next, I was presented with the option of joining a clinical trial. In other words, let's just mask the problem by adding more drugs. Dr. Scribble-on-a-Prescription-Pad added a new anticonvulsant, plus five times the folic acid. It was either that or take five individual one milligram vitamins of folate per day.

I mentioned the MRI I'd gone for ten days ago, for which no results had come back yet. He had access. While standing in the doorway of the examining room, without warning me or telling me to sit down, he blurted out the report: "It's grown. I think it has to come out. It's not going to matter how much I increase the dose or how many medications I give you to try; it's not going to stop the seizures because the tumour is pushing on that part of the brain."

I sat with my hands under my thighs. My ankles bounced around like they had a nervous habit, unable to contain themselves. I was stunned to hear the tumour had grown, as the last three MRIs had showed no growth. This called for drastic measures. I had it in my mind that I would deal with the problem by Dr. Sumnerve's recommended "watch and wait" philosophy. I'd hoped not to have a biopsy, let alone brain surgery! I was befuddled; I listened to what the doctor said, but I didn't really *hear* him. As important as his words were, my mind was racing. I fought back the tears.

I did manage to squeak out that Dr. Sumnerve had admitted to me that tumours weren't his *expertise* and he didn't want to operate, in case he accidentally made it worse. In my case, he figured the cons outweighed the pros. According to him, a total excision wasn't always possible and the tumour would likely regrow, but at a slow rate. But he had also snuck in a sentence of good news: "Once removed, it may not become symptomatic during the patient's lifetime."

I expressed these concerns to Dr. Neurotron. "If this is the case, I don't understand why I'm even seeing Dr. Sumnerve in the first place; his idle hands are no good to me." My heart pounded inside my chest. I wrestled with tears. I had a lump in my throat as big as a toad's as I croaked out, "How am I supposed to deal with some freaky, debilitating thing in the most complex organ in my body?"

"Would you like a consult for a second opinion?" he offered.

"Absolutely," I said without hesitation.

Dr. Neurotron assured me he'd get me in to see another neurosurgeon. When he told me he would refer me to see Dr. Flawless, I was relieved, as I had heard nothing but rave reviews. He was known to be the best in the business.

As I exited the office, I realized I'd have to say farewell to Dr. Sumnerve's secretary as well as Dr. Sumnerve himself. She was never rude or impatient and was always quick to return my calls. She was very understanding and accommodating. "I don't care if you call a thousand times," she'd say. "Whatever you need, just call."

## Popping Pills

I had advanced from a small pill bottle to a medium one, and then jumped up to super-sized plastic cylinders. I had to take three in the morning and three at night, along with a few other vitamins. These suckers were like horse pills and I was always scared of choking. I'd hate for one of these to get caught in my windpipe.

I sometimes got flashbacks to when I was a kid. I'd been sucking on a hard candy—butterscotch, to be exact—when it got stuck in my trachea. Somehow I'd managed to spit it out and catch my breath. Due to this traumatizing experience, I had to psyche myself up every time I needed to swallow a pill.

First I opened the pink pill pack—you know, the ones seniors use so they don't get their days mixed up. Well, I'm the proud owner of one of those cases. My pills were organized in their own little compartments. That way, I wouldn't have to ask myself in my old lady voice, "Did you remember to take your pills, Angela?" At least I didn't need a blister pack. Yet.

Alex once told me I looked like a turkey when I took my pills. I'll admit to doing some weird things with my face; I feel it, but I can't control it. After taking a swig of water and swishing it around my mouth, I lean my head back and squeeze my eyes shut. Down the esophagus the pill goes, riding the waterslide into the pool below.

Alex would split a gut as he watched the whole ordeal. I had to turn around so he wouldn't make me laugh. Once all the pills went down the slide, I'd turn around and face him. "All gone," I'd say, opening my mouth.

Alex looked at me like I'd escaped from the funny farm and said, "It sounds like you have a mouth full of marbles!"

Just a spoon full of sugar helps the medicine go down. Now I understand why the vet advised me to put jam on the pill when I had to deworm my pup. I also recollect the vet tech telling me to smooth my hand under my cat's chin after giving him hairball medication. After treating him, he would eventually cough up a big ball of hair. I had to try these helpful hints to help me swallow my own pills!

## Meds Gone Bad
*October 8, 2011*

That October, I had relatives flying in from Calgary. After picking them up from the airport, we proceeded to drive from Saskatoon to my hometown. My cousin, her husband Michael, and their adorable daughter Clare all packed into my car. When the opportunity arose, I let Michael drive.

A major downside of this obstacle in my brain was that I was apprehensive about taking long road trips on my own. It was pretty upsetting that I couldn't visit my parents whenever I wanted, like I had done before.

On account of increasing my usual dosage, along with starting to take a new drug, my body decided to react. The neurologist had told me about the new drug's possible side effects: drowsiness or dizziness, nausea and vomiting, blurred vision, poor coordination, and clumsiness (ataxia). I was also supposed to tell my doctor if my seizures persisted, changed, or worsened.

On this particular road trip, I had a seizure every hour on the hour. My body was acting as though it had its wires crossed. We stopped to get fuel, but when I started pumping the gas my body had other ideas. My hand trembled and my leg went weak. I didn't have enough strength to hold the nozzle, so Michael took over. I slumped back down in the passenger seat without yelling "Shotgun!"

As I stared out the window, I realized that my seizures were worsening. I could see my quality of life slowly going downhill. Yet no matter how bad the situation seemed, I always tried to look on the bright side—in this case, that meant my fuel bill was taken care of.

By the time evening rolled around and we arrived, despite trying to have a good visit with everyone, I started to fret. All I could think was, *Please don't let me end up in the hospital.* My last episode at the Weyburn General Hospital, back in 2007, flashed before my eyes. My doctor had left me on the backburner all these years. It had been her responsibility to keep her word, but she never had made the call to a neurologist.

I clasped my fingers together and dropped my elbows onto the table, a muddled look on my face. That evening, a new symptom was bestowed upon me: paraesthesia. I started having a "pins and needles" feeling on the bottom of my right foot. I shook my limb, trying to wake it up. After the tingling and prickling went away, I stood up and was rendered speechless.

I took my newbie drug for two nights before quitting. I also cut back the dosage of my other drug, from three pills to two. The new formula was probably the culprit.

Three days later, the visit soon came to an end, and hurray! No hospitalization for Angela. My condition was back to stable, but I didn't like playing head games. I was happy to be on my way back home to what we Saskatoonians call our city—Toon Town.

## You Little Copycatter

Alex and I, along with the rest of the Calgary clan, went out to one of our favourite restaurants: Fuddruckers—Fudd's, for short. Their flapper pie was second to none.

I had a lot of fun with Clare, who had just turned two. At that age, she'd repeat everything I said. Truthfully, this two-year-old was as bright as a shiny sports car. I called her my little genius. I knew she could speak clearly, otherwise I never would have messed with the word Fuddruckers.

Clare enunciated her words and spewed them out fast in her adorable little voice. I also got her onto the word Fuddcluckers (chicken strips). Then I went one step further and showed her the yellow bottle with the words "Mother Fuddruckers Mustard." She copied it clear as a bell.

If I had been guaranteed to have a little munchkin like her, I might have considered having a baby, but they just don't make 'em like that often enough.

After overstuffing our bellies, we walked over to Ruckers, a glorified playroom for children, teenagers, and big kids—like us. Nostalgia booted me in the face when I noticed a game I'd played as a child: Operation. There was a name I didn't like to see, hear, or read. It reminded me of the glob in my head that needed to be resected. I shoulder-checked and found a means of relieving my frustration: Whack-A-Gopher. Perfect. I grabbed a padded mallet and laid a nasty beating on those rodents.

As the moles popped out of their holes, I thumped them some good ones. "There, take that, and that!" I yelled like a psychopath, clobbering the bucked-tooth varmints on their noggins, beating their brains out. "You're going to have a throbbing headache in the morning, boys. You better have codeine on hand—a little somethin-somethin to take the pain away."

Alex looked worried, like I had a chemical imbalance or something. "What did those furry creatures ever do to you?" he asked.

"Nothing. They're just in the wrong place at the wrong time." I gave him a devilish grin.

He covered his head, afraid he may become my next victim.

"Don't worry, everything's kosher," I said calmly. "Where are the others?"

"Ready to go."

We sauntered over and made our escape. Laurie inquired if I had tried a game.

Alex butted in and told her I'd been smashing heads in like I'd missed my dose of Prozac. "Those little gaffers didn't stand a chance, the way she walloped them."

"Sounds like you had lots of fun," Laurie and Michael said in unison.

"Oh yeah," I said. "I pounded all my anger and frustrations out. I had to prove a point, that my right hand still had enough strength to beat the snot out of them."

## I'm Not Gonna Take It

On a prior appointment, Dr. Neurotron wrote me a prescription for Clobazam. I read the side effects: drowsiness, drooling, and possible addiction.

*I'm not taking this junk,* I told myself. *I don't want to be sleepy; I don't want to be like one of the seven dwarfs.* I skimmed over the prescription again and noticed that he had started me out at ten milligrams. For the first week, I was to take it once at bedtime, then twice a day thereafter. *No way, Jose.*

This was a pharmaceutical used to control panic attacks. Any normal human being would be a little on edge under the circumstances, but I wasn't about to take any more pills. I wouldn't risk having to admit myself into the Betty Ford Clinic.

Apparently, Clobazam is used to treat seizures, and studies show it gets along with my other drug, Keppra. I forbid them to even get acquainted, let alone become buddies. The Keppra was coping fine, flying solo.

When I went to my follow-up appointment with Dr. Neurotron, the secretary asked if there had been any changes to my medication. I confessed that I hadn't started the new pills.

She instantly became abrasive. "You have to trust the doctor."

I assured her that I'd let him know of my lack of obedience. When I got to the exam room, I came clean. I told him I didn't agree that I should take these because of the side effects. I mean, come on… drooling?

"Nonsense," he replied.

I grunted. He wasn't the one having to pollute his body.

## Pharmacy 101

I was becoming frustrated with my neurologist. Why couldn't this man help me? Instead he just prescribed different meds, explaining that one was a cousin to another and so on and so forth. I didn't give a hoot about drug genealogy. Wouldn't it make sense to give me sample packs of the "related" drugs until he figured out who got along with who, without causing a family feud? All I wanted was for him to get to the root of the problem. Did I have to spend dollar after dollar on medication that didn't do a bit of good?

I noticed I was running low on pills, so I went to the pharmacy and asked to have my prescription refilled.

"Which ones?" she asked.

*Oh boy. That's not a good thing. What's next… bubble packs?*

"I'm not following the doctor's orders, so I'm back to taking two, twice a day, not three. And that other junk he prescribed, well, what do you recommend I do with them? I was going to throw them across the room, or perhaps directly in the garbage."

"We don't recommend you throw them out," the pharmacist said. "We would like you to bring them back so we can dispose of them properly."

I had no idea what she meant. Did they go into an incinerator? Did they jackhammer them, or what? It didn't matter. She went on to say that they didn't like the pills to end up in the ground.

*You don't want them in the ground, hey? Well, just think how I feel about having them in my bloodstream, making me worse off than I already am.*

The voice inside my head was screaming so loud I could hear my ears ring. I had to tell myself to calm down; it was easier said than done, though.

Angela Freriks

## Don't Shoot the Messenger
*October 13, 2011*

We followed the big blue "H" sign for a second opinion with Dr. Flawless. Alex and I headed down the hospital skywalk. As we walked down the corridor, I noticed the walls were painted with clouds, and below the clouds were inspiring words: "Courage, Strength, Peace, Trust, and Hope." As I sauntered down the walkway, gripping my cup of coffee, my knuckles whitened.

*Buckle up, this might be a rough ride*, I told myself.

I wondered what this new dude had in store for me. Actually, I shouldn't refer to him as a *dude*. My apologies. I should have the utmost respect for this man, the top banana. Neurosurgeons sometimes have a reputation for being arrogant know-it-alls, which was fine with me. I was all for a confident neurosurgeon. Thus far, no one else had come up with any answers for me.

*Oooh, here comes the kingpin now.*

We introduced ourselves and he pulled up the image of the foe in my brain. Much to my surprise, he had an excellent bedside manner. He didn't have an air about himself at all. He seemed down-to-earth and talked to me on a level I could understand.

I told Dr. Flawless all about my situation, how I was living with a repeat offender who was quickly becoming exhausting. As I told him my story, I found myself staring at his hands—the skillful hands of a surgeon. You can't put a price on those. Those hands had to have been insured for big bucks. Maybe a million a mitt. Just think if a waitress, not knowing who this man was, accidently spilled hot coffee on his hand… they looked so perfect, so well-manicured and soft, completely hairless, not one single follicle to be found. It had to be those latex surgeon gloves he used.

My focus snapped away and I looked him directly in the eyes. He asked if I was still driving. I replied with a coy, "Yeah." I could feel my heart pick up the pace. The time had come. He looked at me, shook his head, and said in a soft yet firm voice two words which I will never forget: "Not safe." He proceeded to tell me that he would have to contact SGI (Saskatchewan Government Insurance), that it was his legal responsibility to do so.

My immediate reaction was shock. I hated to admit it, but I was fixated on my own less-than-perfect hand, and it wanted to slap him right across the face. *Kapow!* I sat there straight-faced and knew it was for my own good, but his words were like nails on a chalkboard, making my jaw clench and my body stiffen.

"How am I supposed to get to work?" was my first question. The second followed quickly thereafter: "Am I supposed to take the bus with all my cleaning supplies? You're telling me I have to reconstruct my life?" My voice cracked.

*Maybe I'll have to apply for disability.*

I was at a complete loss. I had joked about how I could be a bartender and make a mean martini, with my hand having a mind of its own ("Those drinks are shaken, not stirred," I'd tell my customers). But I wasn't a people person and didn't want to be exposed to bar flies.

He suggested I look for a different line of work.

That made me defensive. *Listen here, flawless paws. I've had my own business since graduating from high school. Cleaning is what I love. How dare you think you can take away my occupation after serving clients for over twenty years? You cannot and will not take that away from me, too!*

Dr. Flawless didn't think the tumour was in an ideal spot, but he believed surgery could be done. He wanted another doctor, Doc Martens, who specialized in seizures and epilepsy, to be present as well.

"You don't have to decide today," he told me. "But there's no sense waiting a month or two."

In a disgruntled tone, I said, "I'll get back to you when my brain decides what it wants to do."

"Fair enough," he said, with no laughter on his end. I guess brain surgery is, in fact, a serious topic.

"Will I be awake?" I blurted out. "I've heard some people need to be alert during the procedure and I'm pretty sure that isn't going to work for me."

He said he'd have to double check with the other surgeon, but he figured I *would* be asleep. "Sometimes we need to keep the patient awake if we're dealing with affected areas near the senses. In your case, we'll be working in the area that affects your right leg and right arm. I don't think we'll have to worry about the speech aspect," he remarked, showing little or no emotion…

I was speechless.

Needless to say, I thought it would be in their best interest to put me out cold. Some things are just too disturbing, especially if it's happening to you.

I'm not a superstitious person, but I'll never forget that very unlucky day. October 13, at approximately 9:30 a.m., when my life seemed to come crashing down on me, even more than it already had. I had mixed emotions of anger and upset. I barely made it out of his office, walking past all the people in the waiting room and heading towards the exit. It suddenly hit me like a ton of bricks… *bricks* that I somehow felt I needed to lean against on those hospital walls. I covered my face with my hands as tears streamed down my cheeks. I somehow gained control of my emotions, wiped away the tears, blew my nose, looked at my husband, and said a solemn, "Let's go."

You know you've been to the hospital too many times when you start recognizing faces. Lo and behold, there was the couple who directed the brain tumour support group. October was brain tumour awareness month and they had a booth set up. As the man handed me a bunch of pamphlets, I told him about how I'd just lost my license.

Then, out of the corner of my eye, I saw my friend's husband, who worked at the hospital. He was heading my way, so I stopped him in

*Cuddling with Ernie in my rocking chair*

*May 1996 - Bringing home my puppy, Sheena (my K-9 alarm system)*

*September 13 - my unlucky day*

*Mom and Dad*

*My score on the Bookworm computer game*

*March 2009 - Popping out of the sunroof in our limo outside "a Little White Chapel"*

*March 2009 - Madame Tussaud's wax museum (Las Vegas) Dwayne 'The Rock' Johnson*

*March 2009 - Newly weds after tying the knot in Las Vegas*

*August 23, 2011 - I give Lynn Valley two thumbs up! - North Vancouver, British Columbia*

*August 24, 2011 - Climbing for a cause up Grouse Mountain - North Vancouver, British Columbia*

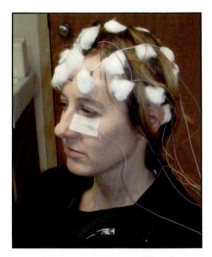

*May 2010 - Getting Wired!*

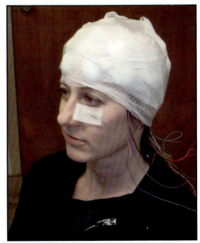

*May 2010 - It's a wrap!*

*I just want my life back!*

*Divine guidance - The Great Physician, guiding the surgeon's hand*

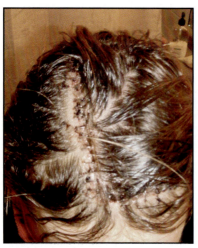

*December 5, 2011 - Me and my splitting headache!*

*Happy and back to normal*

his tracks and told him my recent news. He was very kind and gave me one of those double taps on the shoulder, wished me well, and assured me he would continue praying for me.

## Driving Me Bonkers
### *October 21, 2011*

Over the course of the next week, it was all I could do not to get behind the wheel of my vehicle. It was like a battle between good and evil. I presumed Satan was out to tempt me. His voice reverberated in surround sound: "Oh, come on. What have you got to lose? *Technically*, you still have your license. You yet haven't received a letter stating the restriction is in effect. It's only a ten-minute drive. Just take the back road like you usually do; the traffic is next to none. Why waste money on taxi fare?"

There's a fine line between right and wrong—and, in my case, between the left brain and right brain. The mass was located in the centre, making me think I was in trouble either way. The two sides were right smack dab in the middle of an argument—a brain battle. Not wanting to cross the line, yet not wanting to back down, the right side of my brain tried to solve the problem. Then the left side of my brain was the voice of reason. It pleaded with me not to be stupid, saying, "If something were to happen, you might regret it for the rest of your life. Losing your license for a while is a small price to pay. It's just for now."

My brain stalled amidst all the confusion.

It was getting close to nine o'clock and I had to decide how I was going to get to work. My mind was made up: I was going to drive, just this once. I reached for the keys and my hand started to tremble, making me have second thoughts.

*No, maybe not.* "Okay, Lefty, you win."

I called a cab. As I waited, I stared outside at my vehicle and fought back my emotions. Throughout the cab ride, I looked down at my car keys; all I could do was hold them.

Once at work, I headed down to the basement. This client had a snake, held in a glass terrarium. Their son had moved out, but the snake still resided there. I had rehearsed some words for the serpent. He was hiding under his rock, so I never actually spoke to him face to face. I was pretty sure he was ashamed because he had been defeated. I'd won the battle of evil temptation. I didn't take Satan's bait, and for that I was proud. I smirked at the snake and accepted the fact that life wasn't easy. God didn't promise our lives here on earth would be free of troubles; what mattered was how we chose to deal with our problems. My mom liked to quote a verse from the Bible which means, paraphrased, "Don't worry about what tomorrow has in store, for it is enough to try and handle today's problems."

It was a balmy twelve degrees in Saskatoon. I took advantage of the nice weather (for late October, anyway) and I took the liberty of walking home. That said, it took most of the afternoon to accomplish this. I could sense the snake, with forked tongue, slurring, "Told you to drive. You could've been home hours ago."

I'll admit there was no easy way to get home. I had to be my own GPS system. Since I was hoofing it, I programmed in the econo route. I constantly told myself in a computer-generated voice, "Recalculating, make U-turn on right." It was as though I was caught in a current, being swept in the wrong direction, heading further and further from my destination. First, there was a chain link fence in front of trains. Then I was led to an industrial area with no sidewalks. Finally, I saw a light at the end of the tunnel. After walking miles out of the way, I saw Central Avenue. I made a right and headed down to a nearby Robin's Donuts. As I approached, a man was waiting for the bus. I smiled at him and he commented on what a beautiful day it was. I agreed and added, "Especially, for those of us who have to *walk*." With that simple sentence, I felt like we had made each other's day. He told me to have a wonderful day and I wished him the same.

I deserved a coffee and cheese biscuit. Exhausted, I sat down and let out an involuntary sigh. I placed my bag of belongings on the chair next to me. As I drank my coffee, I continued to observe the people outside the bus stop. I noticed a very ordinary couple who, perhaps, weren't well off. Despite the appearance of their inexpensive attire and the likelihood that neither owned a vehicle, they seemed legitimately happy. They were laughing, goofing around, and she was fixing his hair. A smile appeared on my face as I took another sip of coffee.

\* \* \*

Besides our neighbours on each side, who were mighty neighbourly, I didn't find our neighbourhood to be at all friendly. I found them to be quite pompous. In fact, it was as if their noses were so far up in the air that they didn't even notice I was there. Some days I felt like a ghost. I could walk by people on the way to the mailbox and not receive a hi, bye, nod—nothing. Maybe I should have jumped out at them and shouted "Boo!" just so they knew I wasn't an apparition.

When I got home, I looked in the mirror and saw that there was, in fact, a reflection. *Whew, not a ghost.*

## Numbskull

The most disturbing thing was brought to my attention: in order to remove the tumour, the surgery was going to be rather invasive. My particualr tumour was deep down inside and they'd have to go through a canal to get at it. Sometime before, Dr. Sumnerve had reassured me by saying such surgeries had been done before. *Well, I should hope so.* Then he went on to say, "But it would be much easier if the tumour was closer to the surface."

Duh. It didn't take a brain surgeon to figure that out!

I'd thought of every question and exhausted every scenario of what they might have to do to me—except *one* thing.

"You *do* realize they are *actually* going to have to saw your head open," someone once said to me. What would ever possess someone to say such a thing?

"Really!" I shrieked. Immediately, I thought of the old saying: *Get it through that thick skull of yours.* My heart started skipping rope, Double Dutch-style. Just how thick were we talking here? Were we using band saw blades? I didn't want to even go there. I covered both my ears and started yelling, "La, la, la, la!"

I just about came unglued. Then I thought about these lyrics: "You say it best when you say nothing at all."

## Whiny Baby

"Quit your whining, kid," I grumbled.

Alex and I had just sat down at our table when someone's child decided to get up and not walk, but leap while heading to use the facilities. As he bounded across the restaurant, his foot got caught on the back of my chair. The klutz sprawled out on the floor and I noticed his lips begin to quiver. He faked a cry.

"Suck it up, buttercup! You're not the one having to get your skull split open," I said, making my exasperation known.

Alex scowled at me, leaned in, and whispered, "Your voice carries. Keep it down."

"Oh, he's a kid, he'll bounce back. They heal in no time."

I'm not that cold-hearted, really, but I wasn't in the mood for a cry baby. He was a boy, and boys play rough. Anyway, he was fine. Not a scratch on him.

## Think Tank

The only tank I was putting miles on was my thinking tank. The fuel gauge was running on empty. Soon I would be sputtering around on fumes. All this thinking and going nowhere made my brain hurt.

## Cranium Crisis

I lay awake at night, insomnia taking over, while chanting: "No cab, no taxi, no bus... no way!" The words seemed to echo. I racked my brain trying to think of every which way I could get to work. I hashed and rehashed everything. I could not, for the life of me, shut my brain off. Think fast! Think hard! I thought and thought deeply about what my new transportation system would be: walking, biking, snowshoes, dogsled, hitchhike, or skateboard. No, skateboarding was out. I was too old a dog to learn new tricks, unless Tony Hawk could be my instructor; I might be interested then.

The neurotransmitter was being disruptive and it needed discipline. I yelled harsh words directly at the tumour: "This is entirely your fault! I've got too many irons in the fire and I'm sick and tired of dealing with you."

I tried sleeping and had no luck. I took a dietary supplement, a night-time sleep aid. My body seemed like it was immune to the stuff; I didn't get the tranquil rest I was hoping for. Sleeplessness gave me the opportunity to write a letter, though. My license, revoked? Oh, heck no!

I retired to my office, sat at the desk, and pulled the chain on the lawyer's lamp, the one with the brass base and green shade. I made a list of points on a piece of paper and jotted down every reason I could think of why I should be allowed to drive.

Dear Sir or Madam,

I would like to bring to your attention that I do not agree with the restriction on my license. My license has always been the straight $25. Now, why is it that I have been driving all this time—four months short of two years—and my general practitioner never said anything? I have seen my neurologist on several occasions and not once did he tell me I shouldn't be driving. This is ridiculous; I just climbed a mountain fifty days ago!

I blinked hard to keep my eyes dry. I crumpled up the letter and tossed it in the trash.

That night, my memory returned to a driving incident several months earlier. My friend, Jody, who had said she wanted to see my hand in action, did get to witness it. I was driving one day when I started slowing down for a traffic light. I was startled when an aura warned me a seizure was coming on. For once, I hoped to get stopped at a red light, but the light turned green. I was stuck in first gear and didn't have the strength to shift down to second. I didn't have control of my leg, either, but somehow I managed to press the gas pedal with my gibbled foot. The whole Jeep jerked and convulsed, along with myself.

Jody looked over at the car beside us, with her hand over her heart. She told me the man driving gave me the stink eye. I managed to pull over safely. From Jody's intense breathing, you would have thought she was going into labour. I looked over and said, "Looks like your Lamaze classes came in handy."

Jody then aggressively merged into my lane of words, peering over her shoulder. "My suggestion, *Mrs. Clean*, would be to use your broom and fly to your clients' houses."

I smirked at the image. "My livelihood depends on having a license. I need to be able to get around the city."

"You could pull a little red wagon with all your cleaning supplies behind you and change your business name to Immobile Maids."

I half-cracked a smile and shrugged it off. "Hardy har har. Very funny. Well, there you have it," I affirmed. "The proof is in the pudding. That's what happens when the nuisance in my noodle starts misbehaving. Well, that's that. Good to go."

And we were off.

Reality then set in.

*Listen, there's a possibility that you'll need brain surgery,* I told myself. *So just let it go.*

Cranium Crisis

## Remanded into Custody

I surrendered. I walked up to the front desk of the license issuer like I was going into remand before sentencing. I handed him my driver's license. That was my ID, who I was. I felt like I was giving up my identity as well as surrendering my independence. I felt like asking if he needed to take my belt and shoelaces from me, too.

I was being sentenced for a crime I hadn't committed, but I had to do the time anyway. How long that time would be… I didn't know. I guess I'd have to wait and see if I got paroled. Some said it would be up to a year; others said I'd have to be seizure-free for three consecutive months. Worst case scenario, I may never drive again, if the seizures didn't stop. Only time would tell. In my opinion, I was serving hard time.

I certainly felt like a big part of my life had been taken from me. For those of you who've never had this happen, you'll never fully understand. I did nothing to deserve this, but out of this I tell people never to drink and drive. Believe me, losing your license sucks.

## Yo, Cabbie!

I jumped into the backseat of a cab and wasn't in a talkative mood. I had a mad on. I must've been standing at my door for darn near half an hour. I hated wasting time waiting. Finally, I saw a bright yellow car approaching, so I swung the backpack over my shoulder and armed the alarm.

"G'day," the driver greeted with an Australian accent, which I thought was odd because clearly he was a Canadian chap. My first impression was that this mate was a total dweeb and his bad accent left a lot to be desired.

Right away, he bombarded me with questions. "So, you don't have a license?"

"Nope." Nuff said.

"How old are you?" He crinkled up his eyebrows and I noticed he was peering at me in his rearview mirror.

I frowned. *If it was any of your business, I'd let you know.* I did, for some reason, spill the beans about my age.

"I thought it was bad that my son doesn't have his license, and he's twenty-six!" he exclaimed.

"Oh, for crying out loud. It's this medical thing I have!" I snapped.

I was so sick and tired of talking about it.

He wasn't getting much feedback, so he must have gathered I didn't want to discuss it further. He changed the subject and his words went in one ear and out the other. He was wasting his breath.

The ride seemed to take forever.

*Just shut up and drive,* I thought.

At last, we approached my destination. I was so frustrated because I had specifically asked the driver to take a different route. He ignored my wishes, as if to say it was his way or the highway. Maybe it was my imagination, but it sure seemed like he thought he was king of the road.

A tip? Take a wild guess. Zilch. I handed him a twenty, then sat there with my hand out while he counted the change. I pocketed the money and slammed the car door shut.

## Taxi Amigo

The next two times, I fortunately got a different driver. My nose was pleased with this man's soothing cologne. He was young, friendly, and didn't ask questions; this time I was the jabber-jaws. That was out of character for me. Usually, I didn't speak until spoken to, yet my lips flapped a mile a minute.

"Did you know that if I took the bus it would take me almost two hours to get to where I need to be?" I said.

He smelled great. My noise was pointed up in the air. I felt like a dog, following the aroma of a freshly barbequed steak. I yattered on about whatever came to mind. Senseless chatter.

I was headed into the ritzy part of town. I described the house I needed to be at and laughed out loud. I had been about to say, "I need to be at the big one over there," but I caught myself. All the homes in Briarwood, around the pond, were as big as mansions. They were the *crème de la crème* of real estate.

I pointed to the monstrosity of a house and he pulled over, stopping the meter.

"*Gracias, amigo,*" I said with a wave.

## Caution Pedestrians

I couldn't believe the drivers here in the Bridge City; they zoomed around like maniacs. Everyone's in a hurry and few vehicles ever stop to let pedestrians cross. I'll have you know that we do have the right of way, and the signs are pretty clear.

While Alex and I were out cruising one day, we came to a crosswalk at a four-way stop. We just about witnessed a pregnant lady get hit. A young girl in a car came flying up to the stop sign. She didn't stop, though, and slammed on the brakes, missing the mother-to-be by inches. The girl driving just covered her mouth with her hand. We could tell what she was thinking: *Oops, my bad.*

On another occasion, I was out with some friends for a stroll through the park. They were both pushing strollers. We literally stood on the curb, already in the crosswalk, and not *one* Good Samaritan stopped to let us cross. Unreal.

Even the buses are on a schedule, and be forewarned: they may not stop for anyone on foot. You have to look both ways before you cross the street or chances are you'll get hit by a bus.

Now that I was forced to walk, I noticed the aggressive traffic even more. Here I was, weighed down with the burden of my furry foe and a backpack. It was extremely icy, and I was afraid of slipping and cracking my coconut. I knew the roads were slick, too, so I stood on the sidewalk and waited for all the people in their warm, cozy vehicles to pass me by. I was bundled up like an Eskimo going spear-fishing.

"And get off your cell phone!" I muttered under the scarf covering my face.

I thought about purchasing one of those crash test dummies. I'd pretend to walk out in front of a vehicle, then throw the dummy under the wheels... *eurch!*

"Dems the breaks! Brakes, use them and slow down!"

I had heard that News Talk Radio host John Gormley loves to get into heated discussions about dangerous drivers. I thought about calling into the station and talking about having a brain tumour. I'd tell him my story of having no choice but to walk or spend money on some other transportation. I'd start the controversy and soon other people would be phoning in and complaining about all the deadly drivers.

Yes, it *is* possible to have road rage from the sidewalk.

## Berry Funny
*October 26, 2011*

Mental anxiety and emotional turmoil physically drained me of all my energy. I was exhausted. My eyelids felt heavy after doing three reps of ten, so I ended my workout.

When I feel asleep, I had the strangest dream. I was lying flat on a hospital bed in a room full of beds. The funny thing was, there wasn't anyone in them. The beds were all freshly made, yet empty.

*Maybe the patients got better and were sent home,* I pondered.

There were lots of people around, though. I recognized a whole swarm of familiar faces in the room, visiting me.

My eyes bugged out as I turned my head and shouted, "Look at this!" Beside my bed was an IV, but it wasn't even hooked up to me and the IV bag was clear—with a big bag of fruit! The bag was full of berries, delicious red berries, not in liquid form but in rather large chunks. What in the world?

Then I noticed a long green garden hose on a spool beside my bed. I got up, unravelled the hose, put my lips around the nozzle, and started siphoning the berries. Eventually, I decided to put a kink in the hose. I figured enough was enough. After all, fruit makes you toot.

I woke up, glad to be in my own bed. I looked around, completely baffled, and shook my head.

## Trying to Pass a Stress Test
### *November 9, 2011*

After Dr. Flawless told me it was his responsibility to put a restriction on my license, I got on the phone with his secretary. I asked her to grab my file, put it on his desk, and let him know that I wanted him to go ahead with the surgery. Now that he'd ratted me out to the insurance issuer, he could go in and retrieve the tumour. That way, I could get my license back.

On November 9, I received "the call." On the other end of the receiver was the harsh sounding secretary of Dr. Flawless. This one was in the wrong line of work. I think she had missed her calling as a warden. Although I'd never met the woman, I pictured a female version of one of those straight-faced soldiers standing on guard outside a castle.

It would've been nice to hear a soothing voice of sensitivity while hearing about my surgery date, which had been set for December 5. My heart started into an immediate cardio workout of burpies, skier squats, and lunges. I felt exhausted and out of breath in no time. I could hardly comprehend what else I needed to do over the sound of my heart pounding. I heard the words: "Blood work," *thump-thump*, "X-rays," *tick-tick-tick*, "stealth MRI," *beat-beat-skip-beat*, "PAC (Pre-Admission Clinic) appointment," *pound-pound*, "…and then you'll need to make an appointment with your family physician and have him or her fill out a history and physical form." *Thud-thud.*

My heart seemed to be pounding out an abnormal rhythm, like pistons going up and down. It was the steady sound of an engine knocking under the hood of an old jalopy. I thought I was going to have a cardiac arrest. My heart was becoming more of an issue than my head.

I got off the phone, and guess what? A seizure—there's a shocker. Involuntarily, my hand began to twitch and shake. It was as though the tumour was upset about the conversation and wasn't happy to hear that it was going to be tampered with.

"You hear that, buster?" I burbled. "You're so *outta* here! I just got word there's a contract out on you."

There was no doubt in my mind that my brain needed renovating. And with this plan of attack underway, I smiled wickedly.

"You have twenty-five days left to live and then you'll be destroyed one way or another!" I told it. "If you're going to act like that, you'll have to pay the consequences. The sooner you leave, the faster I can get on with my life. And I *will* get my license back."

## Strange but True

It was a strange request, but when I saw brochures on research at the Brain Tumour Tissue Bank, I had to inquire. I phoned Dr. Flawless' secretary. Her name was Sheila. I didn't have to be there to know I wanted to wipe the stupid grin off her face. I asked Sheila if she could take note that I wanted to see a sample of the tissue. The line fell silent until I spoke again: "Would I be able to look at it, the intracranial tumour?"

*You know, give it a little peeksy,* I said under my breath.

"What would you want that for?" she asked in a distressed tone.

It's not like I wanted to keep this hideous clump for show and tell. Nor did I want it as a memento; I certainly didn't want to save it to serve as a reminder. Quite frankly, I wanted to block it from my mind. I wanted to examine the specimen causing me all this grief.

I could tell by her snooty tone that she thought I was wacko. Not knowing how to respond, she simply stated, *"Yeah, we don't do that."* Before hanging up, she probably muttered under her breath that I was a nut job.

Hey, you never know till you ask.

I wanted to see for myself the deformity that had been causing me so much misery. This strange phenomenon had been haunting me for almost two years. In the Brain Tumour Tissue Bank pamphlet, I read all about the procedure of tissue preparation and obtaining the fragment in liquid nitrogen at -196°C. The nitrogen was meant to preserve freshness, as tissues undergo rapid deterioration after removal.

That was one bank highly unlikely to get robbed. *Don't write checks your body can't cash*, I thought. I, for one, would be laughing all the way to the bank.

## Scripture Support

In the Bible, there's a scripture that says, *"For nothing is impossible with God"* (Luke 1:37, NIV). It gave me a feeling of peace.

In the beginning, I felt hopeless. Human help wasn't enough. Another hopeful verse gave me strength, comfort, and reassurance to get through this head trauma. It pushed me in the right direction and inspired me to write this book: *"I can do all things through Christ who strengthens me"* (Philippians 4:13, NKJV).

The Bible tells us to lean not on our own understanding, so all I could do was ask that His will be done on earth as it is in heaven. His plans are greater than my own.

Every day, several times a day, I prayed I wouldn't need surgery, but if I did, I knew it was part of His plan. I asked God to be my personal physician, my personal healer. I prayed for the mighty hands of God to heal me completely. I pleaded for the damaged tissues around by brain to turn into healthy brain cells and become new again. I asked that He hear my cries to stop the seizures and allow me to lead a normal life again.

He is the maker of miracles. God doesn't choose to heal everyone, but I felt in my heart that I should share the following miraculous testimonies which I witnessed firsthand.

## Forgiven but Not Forgotten
*September 13, 1988*

Let go of the past. It isn't good to harbour resentment or carry bitterness in your handbag. Sometimes it's hard to erase a horrible image from your mind, like the scene of a bad accident.

Years ago, when I saw my sweet sixteen birthday gift parked in the driveway, my eyes nearly popped out of my head. Talk about wow factor! I cackled and strutted around like a startled chicken that had been grabbed by the neck. I let out a cheer for the whole world to hear! There she was—a 1980 Pontiac Turbo Trans Am with T-tops to boot! On the hood was a decal of a phoenix, a fire-breathing bird with flames exhaling from its beak. The "fire chicken" was breathing onto the turbo hood scoop, and I was turbo-breathing, too.

I got in and fired up my new set of wheels. I cranked up the volume on the Alpine stereo and the music started blaring. The back speakers thumped like a heart about to go under the knife. My adrenaline pumping, I stuck my head out the window, looked at Dad, and asked in a super deep voice, "Can you feel the base?"

He gave me grief. "A little less noise in there," he said facetiously. "Cut the racket!"

One day I made the mistake of letting my boyfriend (I'll call him Andy) borrow my shiny new sports car. While my friends and I waited for him to pick us up from school, I bragged, "Last night I decided to take my car out for a spin. I took the liberty of taking it on the highway for a joyride. I pinned it and got all three turbo lights to glow! She put out seven pounds of boost!"

Andy, myself, and four of my pals piled in. I sat with one of my friends in the passenger seat. Needless to say, we weren't wearing seatbelts. The other three were squashed like sardines in the back. Andy was yelling comments out the window: "Move it or lose it! Quit riding the brake, Geezer! Try using the pedal on the right!" Then he goosed it and we were cruising along at a pretty good clip.

"Ease up on the gas there, Lead Foot Louie," I said, furrowing my brow. Before I had a chance to say another word, I closed my eyes and involuntarily reached for the handle above the glove box. My body flopped forward and whipped back into a vertical position.

I sat there in shock. The first thing I noticed was the hood of my car folded in two. The car was wrapped around a light standard, which was right in front of my face. A street sign had been knocked over and pushed to the ground. I looked over at Andy like I was going to skin him alive! The steering wheel was bent inward from his grip and the impact of the crash. I stared out the shattered windshield and noticed an imprint with strands of my friend's hair hanging down.

I heard sirens as I exited, my eyes fixed on the scrunched car. "Cut the engine," I said, my voice barely audible. I looked down at the scrape on my hand. I walked away from that brutal crash with only one tiny scratch on my knuckle. Three of my friends were treated with minor injuries and released. Evidently, "the driver" had failed to negotiate a left turn. Andy claimed that the throttle stuck. Sadly, I only got to enjoy the car for three months. The fact remained that the car was totalled; the phoenix didn't rise.

I was reluctant to go home. I hung my head in shame. I swallowed hard, figuring Mom was going to have a conniption fit and Dad was going to come unglued. Ultimately, they weren't mad, just glad I was okay.

I breathed a sigh of relief. "I figured you'd freak. I guess it could've been a lot worse, by the looks of the damage."

They agreed: a vehicle can be replaced, but a life cannot. "Accidents happen," they said in tandem.

My parents had to pay the seven-hundred-dollar deductible. Damage to the light standard was estimated at a hundred dollars. Andy was a write-off, too. The only present Andy ever wrapped for me was my car's nose around a light standard!

## Heart to Believe

It was Christmas 1997. My dad had just overindulged, stuffing himself fuller than the turkey itself. After heading up to the trough several times, he decided to go out and play hockey.

While on the ice, he felt flu-like symptoms. He felt nauseous, which was accompanied by chest pain and tingling down his arm. He dismissed this as overeating, followed by overexertion. When he went into the dressing room, one of his teammates commented that he didn't look good. Dad agreed he wasn't feeling well.

Once home, Dad lay down, but he was agitated and couldn't get comfortable. It had been quite some time since his symptoms started, so Mom insisted she drive him to the hospital. They ran some tests, which determined he'd had a heart attack.

A man in his early fifties, in good shape, yet having to go for a stress test—I didn't get it. He was a carpenter by trade and an avid athlete. The man had no fear on the ski slopes. He'd say, "Okay, bro, let's take it from the top." The top, meaning the peak of the mountain… and it was all downhill from there. Black diamonds were his jewels of choice.

My dad was an energetic, ambitious, hard-working man. And at the end of the day, he still had energy for more. In summer, he played softball; in winter, it was hockey. On trips, he didn't seem to know the meaning of the word "relax."

He was up for anything, even if it was climbing all ninety-nine steps up the Mayan pyramid in Chichen Itza, Mexico. Dad had a "no guts, no glory" attitude. He went windsurfing *without* lessons. This wasn't advised, as the Coast Guard had to rescue him from drifting out too far; Dad had been heading towards the coral reef.

While on vacation, he sought adventure and walked, then walked some more. Mom and I would just be starting to roll out of bed when he came back from miles of walking along the beach. The man was truly amazing. He could hop on his bike and ride for hours.

He was physically fit on the outside, yet his cholesterol was high, blocking passages on the inside. While at the hospital, he was told that he'd need to have heart surgery. I couldn't fathom my dad being dealt this card. I was in disbelief when I heard the news. The nurse informed me he'd be transported to Regina by ambulance.

I remember being in his room, breaking down, saying these exact words: "I don't want anything bad to happen to you." After I left his room, I came undone in the elevator. My tears spurted out like water from a hole in a garden hose.

Dad was scheduled for bypass surgery and Mom drove Dad up to the Pasqua Hospital in Regina. After dropping him off, she fled. They told her she might as well leave for awhile because there was nothing else for her to do.

The medical team gave him an angioplasty, shooting dye through his veins so they could confirm where the blockage was. When the results came in, the nurses stood in awe; they called the surgeon in and his words, verbatim, were: "I guess I'm not going to make any money off you today. There's no sign of any blockage. You can go home."

When Mom answered her cell phone, shortly after she left the hospital, she immediately assumed something had gone wrong. As it turned out, it was *Dad's* voice on the other end asking her to come pick him up.

"What's going on?" she asked. "They can't be done already."

"Don't need it," Dad told her.

It is a proven fact that God works in mysterious ways. His amazing grace healed Dad.

I wondered if he sensed anything out of the ordinary the miraculous day of his scheduled surgery. I asked if he felt anything special was going to happen.

"No," he said. "I thought I was going in for surgery and then the doctor told me otherwise."

"Well, God sure cut it close that day," I told him. "Blockage of the arteries doesn't just disappear."

Just so you know, Dad doesn't *do* gravy anymore. It's not heart smart.

My dad has a heart of gold. He treats everyone equally—every race, every human being—whether he or she is at the top of the rung or down on the lowest totem pole. He has a soft spot for people with disabilities; they are all precious in God's sight, as well as Dad's. He volunteers at the Rescue Mission and helps the needy. He's still alive and well today, nowhere near retirement, going strong and continuing to do his work and God's.

## Cancer

My dad had another health scare when his doctor removed a mole on his face. While he was waiting for the results of the test, he was concerned it might be cancer. If his concern had turned into fear, it would've all been for nothing. The tests confirmed it was basal cell carcinoma (BCC).

"This type of cancer," the doctor told him, "is the best kind to have." What he meant was that it's the most common type of skin cancer. It's a slow-growing form, so it was relatively good news.

"Go home and don't worry about it," the doc said nonchalantly.

After having the mole removed, the doctor said he'd gotten it all and there was no reoccurrence.

## That Rock Did Roll

Grandpa (my mom's dad), a true man of God, had two stories of miraculous interventions. In his nineties, he was set to go in for surgery. He had numerous bladder infections. Finally, the doctor sent him to a specialist and the X-ray showed a large stone in his bladder. He was told he would need an operation.

Mom prayed, "Please don't let Dad have to go through this surgery at his age." Other people prayed for him as well.

Grandpa was spared from undergoing surgery. The doctors were astounded when they discovered the stone had disappeared.

"How can this be?" my mom questioned.

She asked God, in prayer, for healing, so now she had to believe!

## It's a Miracle, You See

When my grandpa was younger, he was in a major car accident. An eye specialist told him that his eye was so badly damaged he would never see out of it again. Not even surgery could bring his eyesight back.

Lo and behold, when Gramps went back to the specialist for his check-up, he had vision out of his damaged eye. He told the doctor he could see and said, "I don't suppose you believe in miracles?"

After examining Grandpa's eye, the doctor replied, "Yes, I do, because there is *no way* you should be able to see out of that eye."

God has all the power in the world. Jesus once performed a miracle by rubbing mud on a blind man's eyes, giving him his sight back. Faith is the evidence of things we cannot see.

My grandma was also very much a godly woman. She would sense things. Mom once told me a story about a time when her brother was in a serious car accident. Grandma dropped everything she was doing and firmly said, "Get on your knees. We need to pray."

Shortly after, the bad news arrived that her son had been in a terrible accident, but he was okay. All the angels in heaven must have been surrounding him, keeping him safe. He walked away from a rollover. This man, my uncle, who was a Baptist minister for many years, is now eighty years and counting. He's still going strong and serving the Lord today.

My uncle doesn't mince words. He gets straight to the point. Without a bunch of jibber-jabber, he once told me about a miracle that had been performed. He had been praying for a lady who attended his church. She had cancer in her lung. Due to the location of the tumour, the doctors couldn't operate. Her body wouldn't tolerate chemotherapy, as it made her too sick.

When she went for a follow-up exam, the test results showed there were no signs of cancer. The golf-ball sized tumour had disappeared completely. There was no trace of cancerous cells in her body. He phoned to tell me her story, to encourage and show me that God is still at work today.

## Molars in Strollers

It's a small, miraculous wonder that my husband still has two baby teeth. Usually, children get their permanent molars around the ages of five or six. One of his molars, to this day, doesn't even have a filling! That's rare, as baby teeth have thin enamel. He's in his early forties and his baby molars have never fallen out. It's not very often you hear of this. Alex claims they're more of an anomaly.

It's hard to imagine, at his age, that all four of his wisdom teeth still reside. I'm all about just having them removed and getting it over with. When the dentist told me I should get mine taken out, I went full gusto. "Yank all four of them out at once... I mean on the same day," I clarified.

In retrospect, had I known I would be spitting blood for hours, I might have rethought that. I didn't realize the roots of these teeth are so deep that a crowbar should be placed on a surgical tray! Dr. Toothbetold almost needed to call for a tow truck to get the one wisdom tooth out.

## Like, Never?

My aunt Jannette has never had a headache in her life. It must be nice, not knowing what a headache feels like. This seems miraculous to me. I often suffer through migraines. All I can do is go to bed with a cold washcloth over my eyes and forehead and sleep it off.

Anyone who suffers from migraines knows the excruciating pain involved. Some poor souls have to get a shot of Demerol, or another pain reliever. They can be so bad that you can't even get out of bed, and if you stand up you think you're going to woof your cookies.

## Let My Faith Arise!

In Luke 8:43–48, Jesus and the disciples encountered a woman who had suffered from severe bleeding for twelve years; she'd spent all she had on doctors, but no one was able to cure her. She came up in the crowd behind Jesus and touched the edge of His cloak, and her bleeding stopped at once.

"Who touched me?" Jesus asked.

Everyone denied it, and Peter said, "Master, the people are all around and crowding in on you."

"Someone touched me, for I knew it when power went out of me," Jesus said.

The woman saw that she had been found out, so she told him why she had touched him and that she had been healed at once.

"My daughter," Jesus told her, "your faith has made you well. Go in peace."

Although I didn't suffer any physical pain or discomfort from the tumour, my chief complaint was emotional suffering. This illness was the hardest thing I'd ever had to face in my life. Every time I had a seizure, it came with the realization that I was *not* okay and that I could no longer function normally, which saddened me and threw me for a loop.

## "This Is the Complaint Department. How May I Help You?"

If God had a complaint box, it would be overflowing with ripped-up pieces of paper of my sob story, each signed with my name. I felt overwhelmed, agitated, exasperated, annoyed, and figured I'd hit rock bottom. I felt so bad when I obsessed over my problems. Why couldn't I just ask God once and know that my situation was totally in His hands?

My husband would complain about my complaining.

"If the roles were reversed," I said, raising my voice, "I'd like to see how you would handle the situation. You should be lucky I'm not any worse off. I'm surprised I haven't visited a psychiatrist or admitted myself into the psych ward by now. This feels like a mental illness and could cause anyone, even the strongest person, to end up in some institution. A crisis like this would make even the sanest person think they're going crazy."

Unless you've been through it, no one can understand the feelings or emotional strain I experienced. This ticking time bomb starved me of my sleep. Many nights I lay awake until the wee hours of the morning, staring into complete darkness while I tossed and fretted about tomorrow. I found myself adding "God willing" to the back of my sentences. I was also extra sensitive to what people said to me.

## Downsizing to Two Wheels

I had been driving for twenty-three years. I owned two vehicles: one was a summer car with excellent fuel economy, which sipped fuel, and the other was a Jeep, which gulped gas. I'd been lacking in the common sense department when I purchased that gas-guzzling pig. But it's a great 4x4 toy and it served me well in winter. It was a sad day when I realized I couldn't use my vehicles anymore. I had been downsized to two wheels. I parked my bike in the empty garage stall.

Whenever I hopped on my *bicyclette*, I was afraid I might lose my balance. I felt like a total loser, biking down the path one day when the tumour decided to rear its ugly head. I had a limited time to react. I squeezed the brakes and darn near flipped over the handlebars. I hopped off the bike and dropped the kickstand. After my body completed its hissy fit, I continued riding along on my bicycle built for two—the tumour and I.

I was cycling down a trail another day when I had a premonition. The defect was leaning against my brain, trying to rock the jukebox. I jumped off my bike, fearful of having a crash landing. I imagined what could have been—me lying on my back, like a turtle toppled over, my arms and legs waving in the air, feet kicking like I was riding a bike upside-down. All my cleaning supplies would've been scattered as I lay in shock, desperately trying to flip myself over.

## To Sell or Not to Sell

When my license was taken away, I overreacted by debating whether or not to sell my Jeep.

I had a flash from the past when a "Mom Bubble" appeared and hung above my head. My mother had once told me I shouldn't make big decisions when I was feeling emotional. I remember once having a really bad day at work when I told her, "I've had it. That's it—I quit."

"Never quit on a bad day," she said. "Give yourself time to calm down. Don't make a rash decision and do something regrettable."

Before I decided to throw in the towel, I thought things through. Just like she said, I felt better the next day.

So before putting the "For Sale" sign on the Jeep, I gave myself a few days to think about whether or not that was really what I wanted to do.

The Jeep was parked in the driveway; every now and then I'd take a peek at it through the picture window. A couple days later, I put the "For Sale" sign away. Who knew? Maybe I'd need it yet that winter.

## Wigging Out

As my surgery date approached, I found myself in a state of panic. I was fully prepared to go shopping for wigs, but first I scouted around the house for possible headgear. I rooted through my closet and found a do-rag (skullcap), a baseball cap, and a beret. In the end, I just decided to wear my usual hoodie and keep the hood up. It seemed to be in fashion.

I remembered the time when my mom got the most horrific perm. It was so bad that she drove straight to Regina to a wig shop. The hairdresser had fried her hair to the point where she looked like Doc Brown from *Back to the Future*. Needless to say, she was more frazzled than her hairdo. When she finally returned to the house, I asked, "What took you so long, Miss Piggy?"

Usually *mamacita* wore her hair flat, but she entered the room with more bounce than a fabric sheet. "This is a wig!" Miss Piggy squealed. "You should see my real hair!" Then she grabbed the mop off the top of her head.

"Ah! Put it back on, before Kermit comes home," I snorted.

"Maybe someday it'll be funny," Mom said, her voice cracking with emotion. "But not today."

Mental note: if someone is upset about something, sometimes it may be *too* soon to crack a joke about it.

Anyway, with the pressure of the brain frazzle, I was ready to tear my hair out. I didn't have long flowing hair like Jennifer Aniston, but I wasn't overly excited to have the Mrs. Potato Head look, either.

I noticed a tattoo magazine one day. The chick on the front cover had a buzz cut. I was thrilled to see that this look was in. I presumed I'd be as bald as a billiard ball; I even thought it might be sort of cool to take the hair buzzer to design a pool ball with the number eight on my head. I wasn't amused about having to lose my hair, but at least it was winter. I could throw on a toque and no one would think anything of it.

I also found an old dusty bandana in the basement. I planned to wash it and have it ready to put over my bald head. I was about to do the laundry, but when I reached for the bandana, I threw it back down on a pile and said, "I don't need it."

"You won't need it," a voice inside me confirmed.

## Baseball in the Back
*November 28, 2011*

I woke up with an excruciating pain in my shoulder blade. It felt like there was a steel knife in my back, like someone was inserting pins in a voodoo doll and I was the one to feel all the pain.

It was kind of ironic that I was supposed to be having high-risk brain surgery in exactly a week. I had felt no pain from the tumour, but on a level of one to ten, my back was a nine. I had no idea what the cause was, but it hurt to take a deep breath.

## Bookworm

I'd like to introduce you to a pal of mine. He's my little buddy full of encouraging words and his name is Bookworm. He's a computer game in which the object is to build as many words as you can without burning down the library. If you get a bunch of burning tiles, the worm warns you in a screeching, high-pitched voice, "Watch out!" He's there with me during the game. He wears glasses, and behind his spectacles you can see him blinking. Some may find him to be offensive or rude, because when he chomps up the tiles he has a tendency to burp. Depending on how loud you have the speakers cranked up, this worm can make the desk vibrate. And no apologies are made.

If the bookworm is proud of the word you've created he'll let you know by giving you different coloured tiles. He blurts out words like, "Very good," "Awesome," and my favourite, "Fantastic!" His voice goes up a couple octaves, like he can't believe you spelled such a long word. I sometimes laugh so loud that I find myself talking to my pal of many segments, "I know, right? Totally incredible."

I once connected so many letters that I spelled a monster word. I thought the little green guy must have felt a sneeze coming on, as I heard *ah—ah—*and he spit it out: "Astonishing!" I sat in my computer chair, bouncing up and down like a child who had forgotten to take his Ritalin. I let out a whoop, then cried, "Oh yeah, I rock!" I bopped my head up and down.

*You gotta get out more,* I told myself.

I was prouder than a peacock when I reached Level 102 and was inducted into the Hall of Fame. I was *the* ultimate bookworm, having reached the amazing score of 10,278,930 points. I took a picture of it. I was so impressed that *I*, someone with a brain tumour, could reach such a high score. This felt like a great accomplishment. I was so far from scholarly; I'm surprised I didn't spell *Brian* instead of *brain*.

## Engage Brain

When I first moved to Saskatoon, my husband pointed out, "There's a library over there."

*Pfft.* Library? So what. Me, in a *library?* Never gonna happen. I had always hated school with a passion. In fact, I hadn't picked up a book in over twenty years.

Not long ago, I attended a social function at which I was seated at a table with a girl I had just met. We seemed to hit it off. She asked if I'd be interested in joining a book club. "What's the last thing you read?" she asked.

"Oh, I don't know," I replied. "*Stop*."

She stared at me with a blank look on her face.

"You know," I explained, "the red octagon sign at all the intersections?"

She burst out laughing.

Well, perhaps it was some sort of foreshadowing, but ever since my diagnosis I had changed. Previously, I had very little interest in new technology. I was a novice at all the screens out there. One of the first text messages I sent was to Alex: "I'm outside washing my bbq." His reply: "U R meticulous! :)" Lesson learned. When texting, always proofread before you hit send. I had meant to say: "Washing my car." I was also unfamiliar with most computer lingo. I knew I needed to get with the times. I was stuck in an "I'll pencil you in" world.

My better half told me of a computer symptom known as "the blue screen of death." I shuddered as he explained about the *tragedy* that had happened at work. A coworker of his was in a tizzy when her computer crashed and the blue screen popped up. She was distraught about the loss. My voice oozed with sympathy. Alex was a computer guru, so he'd been able to resuscitate the computer.

All in all, I found myself in a highly unlikely place. It was as though I needed a reality check. I needed to stand in front of a map with a big red dot that read "You are here."

The library! *Who'da thunk it?* I mean, who would have ever thought? Well, the doctors told me to get lots of sleep, not to overdo it, and to never skip meals, since those factors could bring on seizures. That's why I found myself at the library, reading, on the computer, and frequenting the pond. Some things I thought I'd never do, like taking the crust off bread and feeding the ducks.

"Who are you and what have you done with, Angela?" Alex asked the new me.

I would be the first to admit that going to the library was out of character for me. But I went, anyway. Now, don't get me wrong, I didn't head towards the books at first; I veered over to the DVDs. Wow! I didn't know you could borrow movies for free. I love things that are free, so I checked out two DVDs and didn't have to return them for a week.

When it was time to return the movies, I didn't just drop them off in the slot; I went in. I was back in the library and, much to my surprise, I found myself perusing the books. A voice from the past hinted that I should read *Chicken Soup for the Unsinkable Soul*. The library I was at didn't have it, so I ordered it in.

A few days later, the light on my answering machine flashed that I had one new message. It was a voice new to my ears: Microsoft Sam. "Angela (and he even knew my *middle* name) Frère Reeks, the materials you requested have now arrived." I laughed so hard I had to hold my stomach. I pushed replay so I could listen again to the way he had pronounced my full name. It was so hilarious.

*Oh, Sam, you are too funny.*

Rather than suffer from brain rot, I made reading a habit. I turned over a new leaf—or shall I say, *page*—and made a commitment to stimulate my mind. My brain cells have never been so active!

I enjoyed an active lifestyle. I'd never been one to sit in front of the idiot box (television). I had trouble sitting still for any length of time and suffered with the "ants in my pants" syndrome. In school, I constantly shifted my body from side to side, unable to sit still in my desk. As a child, I acted like I had attention deficit disorder. All the other "normal" kids were watching *Sesame Street,* but I couldn't sit down long enough to concentrate on some TV program.

# A Complete 180

I used to be a shopaholic. I shopped until I dropped. I dragged my friend Jody around with me to the mall where I weaved in and out of stores like a NASCAR driver swerving around his competitors, racing to get to the finish line.

Brand name clothes were my biggest compulsion. I had a monumental pile of clothes—and shoes!—all ready for the *Yea* or *Nay* pile. Jody would be my critic. She was very opinionated and I could always count on her for honesty.

I pulled a bathing suit off a hanger and held it up. "What do you think of this?"

"Now, is that an eye patch or a bikini?"

"What? Too skimpy?" I closed one eye and did a pirate impersonation. "Ahoy, matey! Ye may have lost an eye on the High Sea, but me likes what I see with the other."

Nonetheless, I put it back.

"Put your parrot back on your shoulder and let's roll," Jody joked.

I had two double closets when I was a teenager, and as you can well imagine I occupied every square foot of wardrobe space. Dad used to call me "Mrs. Marcos," referring to the shoe and boot collection, which was nothing short of a fetish. I had every kind and colour of footwear—all arranged in an orderly fashion.

Today I've recycled most of my obsession and dropped items off at a second-hand store or given them to charity. I've kicked the shopping habit. I have no desire to purchase any more "stuff." If anything, I need to purge. I now feel that less is better. Instead of toting around lavish handbags, I feel obligated to spend my money on more practical items.

## Show & Tell
*September 17, 2005*

Seeing is believing. Mom and I happened to be on one of our mother-daughter weekend getaways when I had the opportunity to meet Josh Duhamel, flesh and blood—for real! He was in Minot, North Dakota, which is his hometown. He was at the Dakota Square Mall, raising funds for Hurricane Katrina, being the heart-warming and heart-throbbing guy he is.

When Mom and I heard the announcement on the radio that Josh Duhamel was going to be signing autographs, I dropped everything—including my jaw! This was an event I couldn't miss. When we got to the mall, I was weak in the knees. I felt like a paparazzi, snapping photos of my favourite movie star left, right, and centre. I had to capture the moment, literally, so I had proof. Otherwise, my friends wouldn't believe me.

There was a long line-up of fans waiting for the autograph session. That's when I found myself scrambling through my purse to find something for him to write on. He was heading my way, walking towards the area which was roped off for his safety from avid fans like me. I felt as giddy as a teenage girl going gaga over her favourite celebrity.

Hunky Pants was looking mighty fine, standing right before my very eyes! I managed to stutter a few words to him and, out of impulse, basically threw my Roots canvas handbag at him. He signed the back of my purse with a black felt marker. He gave it back to me and I stammered, "I'm from *Can–nad–duh*." The guy made me develop a speech impediment.

I showed my now-priceless bag to my mom and exclaimed, "Can you freaking believe this? *Joshy* signed my purse!"

"Yeah, that's quite something," she said. "I see you'll have Josh on the brain all day."

She was astounded by my enthusiasm, as generally I didn't show much emotion. But that day I was strutting around prouder than a peacock. Coming from a small place, when would I ever again have such an opportunity? I was much obliged to be at the right place at the right time. I was anxious to get home and place my most prized possession in a glass box.

The autograph collectible never ended up in a display case. Instead, I lugged that treasure around with me everywhere I went… I'm not *joshing* you.

## Drastic Measures
*December 4, 2011*

The day before my surgery, I went to the hospital with just a glimmer of hope. I prayed that the stealth MRI I was about to have would show the miraculous disappearance of the tumour. I crossed my fingers as they slid me into the hollow chamber. I hoped someone would come barging out of the control room with a confounded expression and say, "I don't understand; the scan shows it's gone! I can't find any sign of the tumour."

Apparently, it was still there, since they pulled me out of the machine and didn't say otherwise.

That day was all about pre-op. First I had to talk to a nurse. She pretty much asked me all the questions I had already answered, from the sheet right in front of her face. I finally told her I had just been at the doctor's office on Friday; it was now Sunday. I hadn't eaten at a buffet, so my weight should be the same.

I asked her when I had to get my head shaved, but she didn't seem to know anything about it. She handed me a plastic tube of special shampoo. I was instructed to wash my hair with it the next day to help prevent infection. She didn't give me any further instructions, though she handed me a brochure. I felt like I was going into the operation blind. I had been expecting to hear horror stories and risk factors.

Alex and I continued on to the next appointment on my pre-op calendar: getting an EKG (electrocardiogram), a test that measures and records the electrical activity of the heart before surgery. All surgical patients have the *privilege* of getting one.

I was given a robe, sent into a room, and had to remove my clothes from the waist up. I jumped on the examination table and, suddenly, a nurse was slapping cold thing-a-ma-bobs all over me. She opened up my robe and stuck blue patches on my chest. The looks on my husband's face was priceless—and let's just say he knew those patches were cold.

Thank goodness it was a painless treatment. I didn't know what to expect when she mentioned the word *electrodes*. After the test was done, I said, "I was expecting some sort of electricity to get sent through my body."

The nurse snort-laughed. "Honey, if you get a jolt, I get a jolt."

From there, I proceeded to get blood work done. I sat with my elbows resting on my knees, in a trance. I was startled when I heard an acoustic voice call my name. I bolted up and followed the nurse to the "scary chair." The lady taking my blood couldn't get the needle in easily, so she recommended just using my other arm rather than having to "fish hook" it in. When she informed me she'd have to redo it, I rolled my eyes; just as I did this, another nurse walked by and asked if I was all right. Maybe it appeared to her that my eyes were going to roll back into my head. I held a cotton swab against by arm, treating it as though it were a mortal wound, as I mumbled down the hall, complaining about her sticking me like a pincushion.

After visiting several rooms, we reached the last appointment. I went back into a change room and put on another robe—this time for X-rays.

On my way home from the hospital, I thought, *Well then, I guess tomorrow is the day.* I warned the tumour that it had only *one* more day to live.

However, when I got home, I did read a useful bit of information from the pamphlet. I laughed and felt it deserved to be highlighted with a fluorescent marker: "A good rest the night before your operation is very important." As if.

## Be Forewarned

Before I went in for surgery, I was told to expect my eyes to be black and blue from the swelling. "It might look like I got beat up with an ugly stick," I commented. I would have a breathing tube down my throat and an IV in my jugular (so the morphine acted directly on the central nervous system to relieve agonizing pain straight away). I would also be hooked up to other IVs, oxygen, and a catheter.

Perhaps I would also end up in a barbiturate-induced coma. Sometimes this was done to protect the brain during major neurosurgery. The doctors need you to remain still. I heard one guy was stuck in an induced coma for four days after surgery.

I warned my family that they may not recognize me bald and to be prepared for my head to have an alteration: a silver zipper look. I didn't know what to expect after being anesthetized. I warned everyone that I had no idea how I'd react to the anaesthetic. I was also worried I might have some kind of personality disorder and shout out obscenities, as I'd heard stories about this sort of thing happening on account of morphine.

The tumour was coming out and a fireplace was going in. Go figure, we were getting a new fireplace installed that same day. Amongst the catastrophe of my head going under construction, our unfinished basement was in the midst of development. Home and head renos on the same day!

## That's Gonna Leave a Mark
*December 5, 2011*

It was the moment I'd been hoping and praying would never come, but it did. I set my alarm to go off at 5:15 a.m., and I had to be at the hospital by 6:20. The surgery was scheduled for 8:00. I was hospital bound. It was the most terrifying day of my life. To tell the truth, I won't ever forget it. December 5, surgery day—"tumour" being the operative word.

Ready or not, this was the day the tumour must die. I went to the admitting desk—and this time it felt real. All the other times, I had basically been crying wolf. I had to put on one of those hospital bands every time I went for an appointment, but I'd always taken comfort knowing I was free to go after the tests were done. During my other visits, I'd been considered an outpatient. On this day, I knew I'd be there for an undetermined number of days, depending on how things went.

I made it through the first set of doors, directly into the hospital. Believe me, I thought of running… running like a criminal faced with a severe sentence and not knowing how long he may be incarcerated for.

From there, I went to another room where I was prepped for surgery. My abdomen was in knots. A butterfly effect. I was scared and a bit shaky knowing I was going to have brain surgery. It still wasn't too late to change my mind.

*You know, you could still run out of here.*

Fortunately, my brain snapped back to its normal size and I decided to proceed.

I went about my business. I had to put on *really* tight white stockings; I thought about taking them home to hang by the chimney with care, being that it was almost Christmas. Once I had them on, I learned they were to prevent blood clots. I put on some blue scrubs along with a hospital gown and housecoat.

Next, I entered the waiting room where my husband, his mom, and my parents were waiting—for me. Finally, it sunk in that I was about to undergo surgery. I plopped down in a chair, crossed my arms, and scowled. To relieve the tension, I joked, "I'm about to stomp into that operating room and give Dr. Flawless a piece of my mind!"

I remembered my mother-in-law mentioning something about a theatre room—a place where all the med students could watch as the operation was performed. My heart sank and I thought, *When I wake up after surgery, I'm going to have a splitting headache.* It was altogether a nerve-racking experience; I was getting antsy waiting for someone to call my name.

"Angela, we're ready for you now."

I did an about-turn. My family made like soldiers and marched down the hall with me. That's when I said my goodbyes.

Alex was allowed to come with me through yet another set of doors. This was called the holding room, where all the patients waited in a vegetative state—some on sedatives, others not. I expected someone to ask me whether or not I needed a drug to calm me, but no drug pushers seemed to be out so early in the morning.

However, a nurse came to my rescue and offered a warm flannel blanket. I definitely could've used some kind of comforter at that point, so I said, "Oh yes, please!"

She returned with a flannel blankie that she had retrieved from a warming oven. I was as cozy as could be, but ironically I still shook. I surveyed the scene, my eyes peering over the sheet, hoping to spot the light of an exit sign. It was too late. I'd gone through too many doors and there were no windows to escape.

Then we met the anaesthetist and I questioned, to myself, whether he would even be able to put me to sleep. A bunch of surgeons were congregated in a room with glass windows. I started to wonder where Dr. Flawless was, but then I saw him meandering towards us, wearing scrubs. His garb gave both the tumour and me an instant reality check. I coached myself to stay calm, then let the tumour have one last nervous twitch.

"If I go down," I told it venomously, "you're going down with me."

I sat straight up in my chair and cleared my throat. *Crap. I was kind of hoping he slept through his alarm, but God's masterpiece definitely got his beauty sleep.*

My anxiety manifested itself and I went from sitting straight to slumping. The surgeon asked if I had any questions. For a brief moment I just sat there... stuck on stupid. I decided to double-check with the mastermind himself and requested to see a sample of the tumour. He told me they'd have to observe it immediately after the resection and send it away to get a pathology report. He was about to perform brain surgery; he had no time to chitchat.

Dr. Flawless informed me that there was a seventy-five percent chance the seizures would go away. Dr. Sumnerve had told me months earlier that even after the surgery I still might have seizures, due to the damaged nerves.

I asked how long he figured the surgery would take: around two to three hours, depending on how it went. Then, without hesitation, Flawless told the anaesthesiologist how much anaesthetic to give me. Someone else took a marker and drew on my forehead, just to make sure they operated on the right side, no left… on the *correct* side.

## Heebie-Jeebies

There was no other way to put it: I had the heebie-jeebies. I hugged Alex and looked at him with sad puppy dog eyes. I still had the last set of doors to enter. I grudgingly walked through the double doors into the OR.

I quickly jumped onto the cold operating table, still huddled in my warm blanket. Without looking around, for fear my eyes might find some surgical instruments I didn't need or *want* to see, I stared into space. I remember looking up and seeing a funky operating light. I held out my right arm and felt a blood pressure cuff go on. I then held out my left appendage, straightening out the crook in my arm. I had expected to have to count down from whatever number they chose to give me, but I never got that far. After that, I don't remember a thing.

## Brain Fog

While Mom and the gang fussed and fretted, I lay on my gurney, rolling with the big dogs, being pushed into the recovery room.

I must have fallen asleep again because I don't remember anything about recuperating in this room. My husband told me I was in a room with about eight other patients and nurses.

Apparently, Dr. Flawless explained to my family that the surgery had gone really well. He told them there had been minimal bleeding and I shouldn't have too much pain. He also said that the tumour tissue was soft, but they had been unable to remove all of it because it had been attached to arteries.

## Wakey-Wakey

I woke up in the recovery room, opened my eyes, and saw the faces of Dr. Flawless, my husband, his mom, and my dad.

*Where's Mom?* I wondered. I guess it had taken her extra time to muster up enough courage to accept the hideous sight I had warned her about. She was such a worry wart.

Dr. Flawless was checking the strength in my hands and feet when I asked him, with gravel seemingly in my throat, "So, how'd it go?"

Then Mom appeared. She could *not* believe I was talking only a couple of hours after surgery.

The most amazing thing was that I still had all my hair. They'd shaved a minimal amount where the incision was. I looked as normal as *normal* could be, under the circumstances.

## The Sixth Floor

I have no recollection of being transported up to the intensive care ward. This was the sixth floor I'd heard about but never wanted to be on. I was in Room 6315.

I assumed I'd wake up feeling high as a kite. When the nurse asked me to describe the level of pain on a scale of one to ten, I simply told her my head felt like I was wearing a crown of thorns. That's the first thing that came to my mind. My head could certainly relate to *The Passion of the Christ*. The nurse made a comment about how she'd never heard anyone say *that* before. She went and got more morphine and added Gravol to the injection as well.

Later in the day, I met a speech therapist. My mouth was so dry it felt like chalk; I hadn't had anything to drink for so long. Besides that, I'd had a breathing tube down my throat during the surgery, which made my voice raspy and weak. When the speech therapist came to talk to me, *he* was the one who got me an orange juice and ice chips. I thanked him, my voice sounding like Marge Simpson.

He jokingly said, "I don't deliver after four."

"Oh! You work on the maternity ward, too?" I retorted, in a smarty-pants voice.

It took the speech therapist a couple minutes to catch my joke, but he did start laughing. My family was asked if they'd noticed any personality changes since my surgery. They said I was the same Angela. I was happy, because then and there I knew I hadn't lost my quick wit.

Alex fed me ice chips as I sucked on them and they melted away. My lips were so chapped that I had to apply almost a tube's worth of Vaseline to my less than luscious lips.

Towards evening, my supper tray arrived and was put on my table, way out of my reach. I didn't care what I was missing when they picked up the untouched tray of food. Around eight o'clock, I was feeling groggy from all the morphine and Gravol; I couldn't keep my eyes open any longer. I'd close my eyes and open them only to see my family staring down at me. My husband suggested that they leave so I could get some rest. I didn't argue; I was *sleepy*.

Later that night, I tried calling out to the nurse who was sitting behind the desk, but she didn't hear my meek voice. I tried to say, "Feeling *naw–sious*." And that's when I managed to sit myself up, lean over the bedrail, and yak all over the floor. There was no call button, so it was their own fault someone had to mop it up.

After hurling, I lay there and became my own personal trainer. I wiggled my toes and bent my feet up and down at the ankles. I still had on those super tight leotards and another layer of leg bags. The circulation leg wraps had six air bags wrapped around my leg. They were like air pressure leg massagers. To make matters worse, I still had the catheter in. I hoped I wouldn't catch a cold. One violent sneeze and the staples could shoot out in every direction!

The next day, I woke up feeling like I was going to throw up again. This time, the nurse was smart enough to give me a kidney basin. Three times I vomited into this tray and it was full in no time. After that episode, I felt better.

Breakfast came. I choked it down, but ate it all. I had my first cup of coffee, but it tasted yucky. I took a swig, smacked my lips together, but figured I was in no position to make demands.

I asked the nurse if she could take out the catheter, because I'd heard a person could end up with a bladder infection from it. She did as I asked. Good riddance; that was one less nuisance to be hooked up to.

Next, she got me the biggest pair of mesh underwear you ever did see. I immediately conjured an image of me wearing gunny sack granny panties, hiked up higher than Steve Urkel's pants. I decided to instead go commando.

Then it dawned on me that I wasn't even sure if I could walk. I asked the nurse for assistance to help me out of bed. I told her I needed to use the washroom. If she would've been on the ball, she might've come up with a witty remark: "I see, little miss crown of thorns, you're going to be seated on the throne."

This was the first time I had tried getting out of bed since the operation. I must've looked like a calf trying to stand up for the first time. *Easy does it. Steady.* I was frail and wobbly. The nurse escorted me to the bathroom and helped me sit on the toilet. When I was finished, I yanked the cord and she helped me walk back and get into bed. Dr. Sumnerve had put the fear in me that I might end up in a wheelchair, so I was grateful I could still walk on my own. On the way back from the washroom, behind the desk was a familiar face.

"Hi, speech therapist," I said, smiling because I knew I wouldn't be needing his help.

"Hi, Angela. How are you today?"

"Angela's pretty good, considering," I replied. Why I referred to myself in the third person, I'll never know.

I had no idea what I looked like. When I used the restroom, I refused to look in the mirror. The therapist probably thought, *Eesh! I hope you feel better than you look.* I must have looked like I'd been pulled through a knothole backwards. It was the day after surgery and because I was off the heavy drugs (I only requested two Tylenol for pain), eating, and using the facilities, I was able to leave the ICU.

Earlier on in the day, I had some visitors. It was a doctor and some medical students. The doctor asked me how I was feeling. I told him, tongue-in-check, "I threw up last night, *right* where you're standing. But no worries. It's been cleaned up." He looked down at his feet and wasn't amused, but one of his med students had to cover his mouth, unable to suppress a smirk. I snickered to myself when they left the room.

I was then visited by two physiotherapists who got me out of bed; I was the piggy in the middle. They were there to make sure I didn't suffer from weakness in my right leg. I was able to walk, but I moved as slow as a two-toed sloth. They gave me an exercise sheet to help me with balance.

They came back the next day, but I only needed one of them as we toured the halls. I heard her report back to my family that I was improving and she figured I wouldn't need a walker or cane. When she came back to talk, I asked her when I could ride my bike again. She advised me to wait until spring.

One of my friends stopped by with a gift bag. Inside was a pair of slippers with clear, non-slip plastic pads on the bottom. I wondered if she was implying I should get a grip. I started to feel like there was some kind of theme going on here; my mother had given me a pair of thermal woollies with T-max heat and traction. The hospital was ever so kind to supply me with bright red grippy socks that read "De Royal."

## Cranium Crisis

Another nurse introduced herself as Ginger. She dropped off a pamphlet on acquired brain injuries. She had a gentle way about her. She pulled up a chair, sat beside my bed, and spoke to me like I was in the psychiatric ward and had lost my mind. Although I *had* lost a piece of it, just the day before.

I figured she must be a social worker when she let me know I could talk to her, if need be. "You've been through a lot and these times aren't easy," she said, then handed me her business card. I think she was there in case I couldn't cope, but it was much the opposite… now I had hope. The worst part was over.

*Ginger,* I said to myself, *you don't have to worry about me leaving the neuro ward. There's no need to spin your forefingers around your ears, making wheee-yooo, wheee-yooo sounds, making me seem crazy. I don't need therapy. This kid is A-Okay.*

## Private Chambers

As luck would have it, there were no beds available for me when I left the ICU, which was a blessing in disguise. I ended up getting a private room for two nights—what a lucky break. I asked Alex if he had spent the money and requested a private room, but he said no. I didn't want a phone or a TV. We all watched a movie on a laptop, which was wheeled directly in front of me on my hospital table. The first thing I did was yank out the bottom of the sheets; those tucked-in hospital corners drove me nuts. Nuts, I tell ya! It's a major pet peeve of mine, sleeping with my feet constricted, pointing down like ballerina toes.

A nurse disturbed my sleep with a pill I needed to take. I scowled as she yanked on the cord and I was blinded by the light above my bed. "Here's your Decadron," she announced curtly.

"What time is it?" I warbled.

"It's 3:00 a.m." She tapped her foot, waiting for me to swallow my pill.

After the rude awakening, I managed to get back to sleep until the next staff bothered me: a nurse took my temperature and blood pressure. Not long after, another nurse did a blood test. My old medication still haunted me; I'd been a fool to believe I would be able to quit taking it once the tumour was removed.

Just when I thought I could get some shuteye, a male nurse came in and told me that the doctors wanted to do an MRI. A porter would be by shortly to wheel me down.

"An MRI? But I thought the MRI machine didn't like metal. What about all the staples in my head?"

"Good point," he said. "I should double-check with the imaging physician."

It turned out that although my head was fastened shut with forty or fifty staples, the MRI would accept me as a client.

An orderly arrived with a high-end model wheelchair with glossy mags. It was a VIP experience! He picked me up and helped me into the comfortable seat. Chivalry wasn't dead.

I made a sexy whistle sound and nodded approvingly. "Sweet ride. How's this thing do for gas mileage?"

It only took me a minute to figure out he was one of "those guys" who was only good to look at. His body language included a tight-lipped smile; it was apparent he had no sense of ha-ha. I was wasting oxygen, and if I didn't know any better I would've thought he was mute. He wasn't much of a conversationalist, so I didn't bother with an introduction. What would I have said? "Hi, Mr. Porter, I'm Angela, a.k.a. Staple Head. I'm totally pumped about finding out about the measurements of the dooflicky, post-op."

While waiting in my wheelchair, a nurse realized I still had a gown on. She performed a magic trick and slipped the gown off from under the housecoat.

"Good thing I caught that," she said. "It has metal snaps in the back and the machine doesn't like metal." I felt like she was waiting for me to slip her a ten-spot for doing such a thorough job. I never left a tip for her or the valet attendant.

I had to have the usual injection of contrast media into my bloodstream. Normally, this wouldn't have bothered me, since I'd done it several times before, but this day was different. I don't know if it was because they injected the solution into my IV, but I just about had to squeeze the button. It was as though my blood started bubbling in my veins.

Here's the best, or *worst*, way to describe it. Imagine a car battery. Now imagine the battery posts are all badly corroded. Then someone takes the battery out from under the hood and dumps it in a pail of water filled with baking soda. The battery acid starts sizzling and bubbling as it's immersed in the boiling, foamy formula.

First the crown of thorns, and now this painstaking abuse. I knew I was almost finished and had to continue lying still. It was especially important now so the radiologist could get a good image of how much of the tumour was left.

At last, they pulled me out of the machine. I asked if they could remove the IV, as it felt like my arm was on fire. The nurse told me that I better wait until I got back up to my ward and ask the people there. She then changed the subject and wanted to know if I wanted to be wheeled out to the waiting room to watch some TV. I didn't feel up to showing off my new wheels, so I told her I preferred to just sit back and wait. I knew I was a sight to behold. For the sake of all others, I chose to remain behind a closed curtain.

It seemed like I waited forever for the same porter to take me back to my room. I hoped he wouldn't make himself sick looking down at the train tracks on my head. Maybe he was using hand gestures, pointing at my path of wires, hand over his mouth, and trying not to gag. Who knows what he thought. The boy never said a word… Chip chip cheerio, then.

When I returned, it was lunchtime and Alex and the crew were there. I immediately complained about the traumatic experience I'd gone through. Clearly, I was in a bad mood and was using a cantankerous tone.

"Settle down, you old hoot owl," Alex said in a joking manner.

"You *do* realize you said that out loud." I smirked, but couldn't keep a straight face.

Alex left to get a nurse, who figured I didn't need the IV anymore. I waved my arms in the air and shouted, "Woohoo! Every single tube is out. I'm free!"

I transformed from mad to glad in a matter of minutes.

Later that evening, as I was settling in, I was informed that I was going to have to be moved. It must have been around ten o'clock at night and I was stunned. I had grown accustomed to my private room.

"Moved? At *this* hour," I asked, exasperated.

You'll never guess what floor I was moved to. The fifth floor—the maternity ward! The first thing I heard was bawling.

*This is a nightmare!* It was probably the best form of birth control in the world... and right away I thought of Dr. Hicks. If I stayed sane enough to make it through the night, I'd appreciate being thirty-nine with no babies.

The room was like an intensive care ward with our own nurse 24/7. There were four beds; that's three more sick people than I was used to. What rotten luck. I had been given the bed closest to the bathroom. This was *not* a good thing. My sniffer was as good as a police dog's and I don't think the bathroom had a fan. The lady adjacent to me was in the washroom a little too long, and I knew no good could come of it. With a squawking baby down the hall and a stench like none other from the washroom, I turned over so my nose was facing away—but it was wafting. I puffed up my cheeks as I tried to hold my breath. What were the stinkin' odds?

*Who does that? For Pete's sake, if you're going to be that smelly, at least shut the door behind you. Honestly.*

It was so bright and noisy in there. I had already lost a piece of my mind, if you catch my drift, and that's when Poopy Pants returned to her bed.

That's also when I overheard two of my roommates start talking. I was minding my own business, caught between lying down and sitting up in bed, with the curtain closed. The two ladies were conversing back and forth, and I'm sure they thought nothing of it. Have you ever heard the phrase "Think before you speak?" These two were across from each other discussing that they didn't have much of a view. One of them said she had been up on the neurology ward prior to here.

"The brain is a funny thing," she went on to say. "The way some of those people act…"

Before she could finish, I piped up. "Hey, I just *had* brain surgery."

Silence. End of story.

## Pistol Packin' Mama

I was home free. The nurses soon informed me I could vacate the maternity ward… leaving without a baby. I was amazed at my own speedy recovery. While I waited for the doctor to sign the discharge sheet, I asked one of the staff if he could tell me the exact name of the surgery I'd had. I thought I'd heard somewhere along the grapevine that it was a craniotomy. But I didn't know the difference between a craniotomy and lobotomy.

"Let me pull your chart," he said. "Ah yes. Here we have it." He flipped through the blue binder containing all my medical information. He wrote down the name: Left Frontal Parasagittal Crani and resection of tumour. I was bewildered.

*Crani? It must mean craniotomy.*

As memory would have it, back in the beginning while doing research, I had showed Alex a picture of a right frontal. "Oh, gross!" I'd shouted, shaking my hands and acting like a real drama queen. "Look at this!" I never would've thought, at thirty-nine years young, I would have to undergo a crani. I felt like snatching the binder from him and reading all the info so I could just copy it all in my book, but that would have been like cheating and looking in the back of the textbook for answers.

As we gathered up my belongings, the nurse double-checked to make sure we had everything.

"The only thing we're leaving behind is the tumour," Alex gloated, as if to say, "So long sucker!"

And with that connotation, I made a kissing noise… *Mmmwah!* I put my fingertips to my mouth and blew it away, giving Mr. Tumour the final kiss-off. I still wished I could've taken a piece and given it a proper burial. I do believe the tumour owes me an apology for its misbehaviour. I forbid it to act that way again.

## Bye-Bye, Brain Blemish

I was discharged on the fourth day after surgery. I had gone in on a Monday and been released on Thursday. I knew I had to get out of there before Friday, since they didn't release patients over the weekend.

At last, I hopped in the wheelchair and put my hood up. I could hardly get out of there fast enough. I needed to get a prescription for a stomach acid inhibitor. I also needed a steroid to prevent swelling. I don't think I took it soon enough because when I looked in the mirror, I looked like a character from *Avatar*. My eyes looked puffy, like they wanted to join together. Normally, the bridge of my nose is narrow and my eyes are close-set. I looked like an alien. I turned my extraterrestrial neck to Alex and quoted in a space creature voice, "I bring you love."

"Yeah, I noticed that at supper time and thought, what the Sam heck?"

"And you didn't *say* anything?" I said in an unearthly tone, as if he had just crashed my spacecraft.

"Well…" He dragged out the last two letters of the word.

## Visiting Hours Are Now Over

I left the hospital without any post-op instructions. I had absolutely no clue as to what I was and wasn't allowed to do. I thought it was sort of strange for them not to leave me with an information sheet, but I guessed I'd use my own discretion and do physical activity as tolerated.

The day after I was released from the hospital, I informed my mother and mother-in-law that I was going to bake muffins. I lined up all the ingredients, sat down at the two-tiered granite island, and whipped up a couple of batches.

The doorbell rang several times now that I was home. Friends and family dropped by the house, commenting on how they'd gone to the hospital but the staff had informed them I was home already. I was bombarded with gifts. This was better than my birthday!

"Delivery for an Angela *Free Ricks*," I heard a voice say. From behind a bouquet of flowers, a little Asian woman unveiled herself, standing about five foot nothing.

"Something like that," I said, correcting her with the proper pronunciation of my last name.

"Oh, so sorry," she said, but she didn't bother getting it right. Instead she pouted, her bottom lip curling up. "Girl not feel well today?"

I looked around the room absentmindedly, searching for the *girl* in question. I gave my head a shake and replied, "I guess you could say I'm feeling a little under *par*."

She broke into a high-pitched, uncontrollable laughing fit. "You must be golfer. I mad at *cheetah,* Tiger." She shot her index finger up into the air and wriggled it from side to side. "I deliver more of these 'I so sorry' flowers to naïve girl from *cheetah*. She take animal back next month. I make rounds again, same girl, more 'never again' flowers… Men!" She swatted her hand towards the floor, then faced the door and let herself out.

Angela Freriks

## The Mirror Was Not My Friend

"Get that mirror *outta* here!" I shouted as I caught a glimpse of the freak staring back at me. I was bug-eyed with astonishment. It was the fourth day after my brain rebirth. I looked in the mirror once, twice—not thrice—then wrinkled my nose. I did *not* like the reflection I saw. No amount of time or energy could spruce me up.

*Well, well, aren't you a fine lookin' specimen?*

Granted, I was thankful I had hair, but man alive was it greasy. It stuck up in every direction. Looking in the mirror, I laughed when I took a step back into the past. My dad used to rub my head, mess up my hair, and say, "Scruffy! Haystack!"

I was used to my hair being blonde, but with all the gunk they put in it to prevent infection it had become dark, like someone had caked on 10W30 oil. It was parted so all the staples showed. I'd taken a shower the day before, but no one would have guessed it judging by my unkempt appearance. I was afraid to get too close to the staples. Frightful of what I might see, I was like a vole peeking out of its hole come spring.

I took another quick gander in the mirror and thought, *No wonder you were on the maternity ward… you've just had a C-section.* The staples were U-shaped and the trap door they made in my head was in the shape of a horseshoe.

## Staff Christmas Party

Alex's staff Christmas party was the same week as my surgery. He said he would play it by ear as to whether or not he'd go. It was my first full day home and I was still hobbling around the house. My worst complaint was a sore lower back, and I had no idea why it was acting up. I didn't know whether to blame it on me puking over the side of the bed and pulling something, the nurses hoisting me up so I could sit in bed, or from simply lying around for too long. I had no clue what had happened as they shifted me around from slab to slab. They could've dropped me on my head and I wouldn't have known the difference. The surgeon would've had to say, "More staples, please."

Everyone wondered how I was doing. My head felt fine. I had no pain, no headaches, I no longer had auras, and best of all no seizures. It was my back that made me consider another dose of morphine to numb the pain.

I needed help into the shower, so Alex jumped in there with me and started washing my hair. All of a sudden, I told him I felt nauseated; I started thinking about the staples and if one got caught and accidently yanked out—*Floop!* The next thing I knew, I fainted.

When I came to, I was on my knees, slumped over in the shower with the water still running. "What happened?" I asked, disoriented.

Alex told me my eyes had been wide open in a blank stare. "You scared the crap out of me! You flaked out."

"I'm fine, as long I don't think about it. I tend to gross myself out with the thought of the metal loops and my swollen brain. I'm scared of coming apart at the seams. My head has been fastened together with…"

I stopped mid-sentence and stood like a drowned rat, tortured by pieces of wire, bent to bind my skin together.

"I can't believe it," Alex said. "One day you're walking into the hospital and on the outside everything looks normal. Other than the tumour, you're perfectly healthy. Then a few days later, it's like you've been in a bad car accident and have to recover. You have bruises all over your arms, you're walking like a penguin, and I'm surprised they didn't have to reload the staple gun."

I agreed. "I know. I'm all maimed up."

Judging by my bruised and needled arms, I looked like a heroin addict. Talk about adding insult to injury!

The next night, my aunt Jannette and uncle Gord came for a visit and decided to pull an overnighter. I was hibernating in our bedroom when I heard a feeble tap on the door. Jannette tried to coax me out with homemade cookies. I warned her that I looked like the wreck of the *Hesperus*. Without hesitation, she entered the room, gave me a big hug, and passed me a stuffed teddy bear with a big, bright yellow smiley face helium balloon.

Jannette assessed my vandalized skull. In her opinion, the work had obviously been done by a professional.

## Don't Crack Your Cabbage

My mom, in particular, escorted me around, treating me like I was her firstborn (first and *last*, actually). She'd be tinkering around in the kitchen while I tried to read. She'd break in and demand to know, "How's it going in there, Ann? Let me know if you need something." Mom has always called me Ann, since I was knee-high to a grasshopper.

I'd be wobbling around in the kitchen and Dad would shrink down in his chair, noticing that the microwave's door was open. "Don't hit your head," he said. Normally I would have needed a translator, as he said this in Dutch, but I recognized the word he used for "head."

I wasn't about to wear a snowmobile helmet every time I left the premises. I'd hit the headlines wearing a crazy getup like that! Although, to protect my head, I was supposed to wear a skid lid while biking or rollerblading in case I smoked into something, or vise versa.

Over the weekend, my back was killing me. I did my best to refrain from going to the chiropractor. Now, this is what I call downtime: I got down on the floor to put an icepack on my back and do some stretches. It turned out that once I got down on the floor, I couldn't get back up again. I was in agony. Everyone was sitting at the kitchen table, but I chose to remain on the floor. My mom and Alex slid my butt across the hardwood and propped me up against the leather couch. I sat on the floor as though I were in Japan while Mom delivered a meal for me, placing the tray on my lap. More food on a tray… I'd thought I was done with that.

Cranium Crisis

## He Cracks Me Up

Well, I'd had enough. I suffered through the weekend. When Monday arrived, I made an appointment with Dr. Bycracky. I was using my mom as a crutch. My hood was up, covering all the staples still in my head. When I told him that I had just had brain surgery two weeks earlier, he was stunned, as well as leery to try adjusting my back. He asked if the pain was in the usual spot and I grunted, "Uh-*huh*."

He told me he could work on my lower back, but he wouldn't be able to do anything if it was my upper back or neck area. I was as tense as a hippo on a tightrope, and all the muscles in my lower back were huddled together like they were making a game plan. Somehow he seemed to think he helped me out, but to be honest I didn't feel much better. I still felt like I was walking around with a constipated look on my face.

I opted for taking a bath rather than a shower after the last incident. I filled the Jacuzzi tub and soaked in a bubble bath, adding Epsom salts. When I managed to lift myself out, I needed to put ice on my back. I felt like I was ninety years old.

## Owie, Mommy
*December 15, 2011*

Ten days after my surgery, I sat in the doctor's office to get the staples removed. I had been advised to take Tylenol before getting them out. This kind of freaked me out and I felt uneasy about the procedure. Other people, including Dr. Frikker (my new general practitioner), had said it would be painless.

I was concerned about the staples exiting my head. Staples are needed to hold papers together and are driven into doors, but these had been driven into my *scalp*.

When we got to the doctor's office, Momma came into the room with me. I warned Frikker that I had a weak stomach and tended to feel queasy at times; I omitted the shower scene. He suggested I lie down. I tried to think pleasant thoughts as I heard Mom say, "It will all be over soon."

Some of them were, indeed, painful as he pulled them out. I could feel my face contort a few times. Sometimes the ends of the staples spread apart so he had to use another instrument to get underneath. After he was finished extracting them all, he showed me the heap of bent staples in a pile on a wad of gauze. I was so thankful to get it over with. He told me it would be quite normal to have a pins-and-needles feeling in my head.

I thought about my coping strategies, namely using comic relief. "With all due respect, Doc, I'm sure you did an excellent job of removing all the staples, but is there any chance the skylight above my skull could leak?"

After the surgeon had flipped my lid and installed a sunroof in my head it felt like I had a speed bump on my scalp. I tried looking at the back of my head, holding up a mirror. I felt woozy at the deplorable sight.

In the days that followed, my sensitive sniffer drove me crazy. Me and my dog nose! I kept smelling rust, and I knew the horrible odour was coming from my head. It was the most disgusting thing, but I kept busy picking dried blood off my scalp. The tiny wounds had formed scabs.

Mother kept harping on me. "Quit picking!" she squawked.

"But I have a bunch of scabbies that need to come off."

"Well, just leave them alone. They'll fall off when they're ready."

## It's Beginning to Look a Lot Like Christmas

Sometimes I'd noticed a few flakes falling from above as I scratched my head.

"When did it start snowing?" I asked out loud.

As it turned out, the white snowflakes were dropping from my head. Some scattered flurries had landed on my black T-shirt.

Alex laughed. "You better add dandruff shampoo to the shopping list. Your crisis seems to be having a snowball effect."

"C'mon, be nice," I whimpered, shoving the elements off my shoulders.

## I've Got More Time than Money

Being self-employed has a formula. No work equals no pay. How was I supposed to make ends meet? I lived on IV for one day, compliments of the hospital. Mac and cheese wasn't healthy, but it'd do in a pinch. Maybe I should just live off the fat of the land. Not wanting to act like a parasite, yet running out of options, I had three choices: IV, K.D. or Hub–by.

The truth is, the less you make, the less you spend.

Fortunately, Alex had a great job. We were more than okay. Nonetheless, no job equals tons of sleep. I didn't have to set my alarm clock very often; I didn't have a schedule, and there wasn't much on my agenda. Time didn't seem to exist. I didn't wear a watch for almost two months.

I learned that I never had to worry about being bored. One day, when I retire, I know I'll make one fine senior. I don't mind staring out the window, taking it easy, and eating porridge in the morning.

## Exploring on the Bus

With Christmas fast approaching, Mom and I couldn't have picked a worse time to try and figure out the Saskatoon Transit System. Four days before Christmas, there was bumper-to-bumper traffic on Eighth Street and an accident to boot. For a split second, I was thankful to be a transit rider, happy not to be driving in the chaos.

I knew it might be a while before I was permitted to drive alongside Saskatoon's most horrible drivers, so I decided to do a trial run, just in case I felt like I might go stir-crazy from being housebound. As it turned out, house arrest wasn't so bad. Idle hands are the devil's workshop, as they say, which is why I decided to tickle the keyboard and tell the world about my brain tumour.

Being a slacker had its repercussions. Sitting, lazing around, and indulging in Christmas baking caused me to gain about five pounds. I was mixing relaxation with lethargy. I'd been taking life easy, watching lots of movies in the comfort of my own home, and going to the cinema. I spent my time curled up in front of the fireplace; books had become my silent friends.

About a month after the surgery, I picked up a bucket and washed the floors. I gave the rest of the house a lick and a promise, as well.

## It Is What It Is

The pathology report came back and it turned out that the tumour had been misdiagnosed. It had *not*, in fact, been an epidermoid cyst. All the time invested in doing research on this burden in my head had been for nothing. Dr. Flawless called and told me that the report had come back, showing that I had what was known as a mixed tumour. It was believed to be a low-grade tumour (grade two). They sent it away to the University of California for a second opinion. The blob in my bean got to go to San Francisco! That undeserving son of a biopsy was travelling to sunny California.

*Yeah, you better skedaddle, mister, cause if I ever get my hands on you, you're dead meat!*

He told me that if I noticed the Cancer Clinic's number on my phone, not to be alarmed, as my tumour didn't contain cancerous cells. I had no idea chemo or radiation was used for anything *but* those cancerous, glowing cells. Dr. Flawless mentioned that I'd have to get an

MRI in about six months' time to monitor the remnants of the tumour. He reminded me again that they hadn't been able to get all of it since the tumour itself had a fuzzy edge.

*Fuzzy? Like peach fuzz?*

He suggested chemotherapy to shrink the rest, or possibly radiation. If any strange or unwanted materials were left in the brain, there was a slight chance they could turn into cancer cells. Not knowing the size of the remaining tumour, I didn't want to take the risk of it converting to cancer.

Naturally, I talked myself into doing a little research, thanks to my know-it-all friend, Microsoft. My mind hit rewind so I could recall the correct name Dr. Flawless had used. I started typing the name of the tumour into Google. Without any choice in the matter, a photo of a man with a shaved head popped up, displaying his recent surgery. At that moment, I was so thankful that it wasn't until *after* my surgery that I found out the surgeon would have to carve the letter of his choice into my scalp.

My mom was still with me when I got off the phone. "Are you positive he said it was B-9?"

"Mom, it's not like Bingo. It's pronounced *benign*."

Then Alex jumped in, like he was playing some kind of word association game, shouting out the first thing that came to mind: "B-9 Bomber." He had to explain that it's a plane that drops bombs.

"Huh, never heard of it," I said, shrugging my shoulders.

Mom laughed and renamed the tumour non-malignant. Right away she was doing research on the computer. She felt better when she found out it was considered "primary," meaning not likely to recur or spread after removal. She's the type who has to beat the horse till it's bloody.

Angela Freriks

## Snail Mail

Over Christmas, I received an overwhelming amount of mail via the mailbox. Thank you to everyone who sent me get-well cards. Along with Christmas cards, I received letters from the neurologist, the Division of Neurosurgery, and the Cancer Centre. What a way to start out the New Year! I wasn't looking forward to applying more *uneventful* calendar stickers for the upcoming year.

Dr. Flawless referred me to see two oncologists (cancer doctors). Because the operation was over, most people thought my health scare was all said and done. Wrong! Oh, if only it had been the end.

## Summary

Well, what can I say? It was far from a good year. I had more problems than a math textbook. I was denied the simple things: I could no longer jump in my vehicle if I wanted drive-thru. My independence was gone and I didn't want to ask for help or bother anyone. I didn't want to impose, not being the type to inconvenience people. I used my health card more than any other. My credit card went into sleep mode and wasn't swiped or tapped a whole lot. I think my wheels just knew where to go; it was pretty much par for the course. I spent a crap load on parking, and my white Sunfire became known as "the hospital car." How sad.

The best month was December, when I was thrilled to say "*Hasta la vista*" to the inconvenient clump in my melon. I found out that a private hospital room was $120/per night. I don't know if I'd call staying in a one-patient room for two nights a gift, but it was $240 worth of privacy. Had I known they were going to ship my unpregnant self down to the maternity unit, I could have made reservations for a Victorian Suite, which are available for maternity only. Such rooms will set you back $150/per night, but they're apparently fancy schmancy, with a much nicer ambiance than a humdrum hospital room.

Christmas card photos clearly weren't an option for 2011. December had me looking like a mangled freakazoid. Yeesh!

# part three

## Out with the Old, In with the New

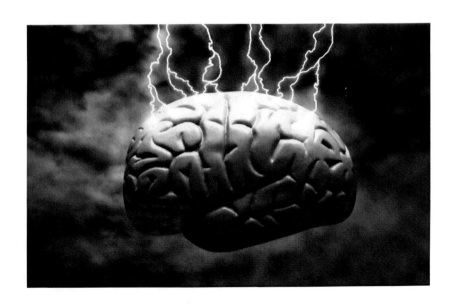

## January 2012

I welcomed in the New Year, knowing that it had to be better than the last. At least I had gotten the main thing outta my mind. I no longer had the fear of brain surgery hanging over my head. The worst was over with.

The weather in Saskatoon was unbelievable. On January 5, we set a record-breaking high with a temperature of 6°C, one degree higher than it had been in 1906. Due to the rare temperatures, it was a shame I still considered myself a recluse.

I was just bragging about how we were having Chinook-like weather when Mother Nature decided to go through menopause. She hadn't been herself these days; while going through *the change*, she took a turn for the worse. The temperatures plunged and frigid cold and snow blanketed the province. Brr! We were in a deepfreeze of depression and had to face the elements that a typical Saskatchewan January might have in store for us. If anyone here can relate to the winter blahs, say "Aye."

Angela Freriks

## Flea & Tick Collar

It had been almost six weeks and I was still scratching my head. My scalp was so itchy. I started to think I needed a collar around my neck to stop the itching. After just getting out of bed one morning, my hair looked all frazzled. Alex joked, "Your hair's all wacko in the backo."

"Jeepers anyway," I muttered as I made my way to the powder room.

When I looked in the mirror, I almost snorted with laughter. The back of my hair was lying down flat, and I noticed tiny little bristles sprouting up from the incision. Little tufts of hair had started to mature. It was almost as exciting as planting grass seed and seeing the results of new blades sprouting up. The pieces of fresh turf were growing in. Aha! And somebody had told me my hair wouldn't grow back over the scar tissue. Thank goodness I would never have to do a comb over!

## Bad Hair Is Better than No Hair

My hair was looking something nasty. The roots came in dark and proud. Finally, I made an appointment to get my ears lowered. The last hairdresser I'd gone to hadn't worked out; she seemed to have been in a hurry and didn't listen to anything I said. This was a bit alarming because I'd asked for a *trim*, not a cut. I immediately gave her a nickname: Jabber Jaws. She did more yippin' than snippin'. Her fingers twirled the scissors around like she was Edward Scissor Hands. I had no idea what she might end up sculpting my hair into. The tips of my ears were frozen with fear.

So, the search continued. I found a new girl at a nearby beauty salon. Normally, I like to get my hair scrubbed in their fancy sink, but I didn't feel comfortable having a new hairdresser lather and rinse my mane, so I washed my hair before I went. It had been almost two months since the surgery, but I was still worried about her raking the comb over my scalp. I told her she had her work cut out for her, since I'd let it grow to an unruly length.

I sat in the salon chair as she butchered my hair. The dead ends were littered all around. I entered the beauty shop with a trio of colours, ranging from dark blonde to almost bleached ends. I left *au naturel*.

## Orientation Station

When I first got the information package in the mail, I opened it, thumbed through a few pamphlets, and slid them across the kitchen table. It was the beginning of a new year. I was still recovering from brain surgery and it *still* wasn't over. I wasn't in the mood to deal with all this Cancer Clinic information.

A few days passed before I begrudgingly flipped open the folder. Inside was a bunch of paperwork I needed to fill out (a new patient health and needs assessment form). I grumbled, but managed to fill in my medical history. Then I perused more papers and found an invitation to the SaskTel Theatre for orientation. I threw the idea around in my head for the longest time, not sure whether or not I would attend. I decided to sleep on it and decided in the end that I didn't think I needed to go.

Alex, knowing how I could get, looked at the papers and figured it would be helpful to go. The invitation said, "We strongly recommend you or a family member attend this orientation session." Whatever.

When I went to set my alarm clock, it still read 5:15 a.m. It had been over a month since I had needed to get up in the morning at any particular time. I had a heck of a time getting out of bed. Alex, my designated driver, picked me up and drove me to the hospital. And so it began.

We took our seats in the theatre. I set down my coffee as the main speaker started the show. As I listened, I didn't like what I heard: on your first visit, you may need blood work; she referred to it as "phlebotomy." Judging from the past, I didn't believe there was such a thing as "you may"; it was always "you will." I shook my head and thought, *You can BS your friends and I'll BS mine, but let's not BS each other.*

I caught the speaker looking over at me a few times and knew I had a scowl on my face. It was legendary how much I despised blood work. I didn't want to educate myself, using their medical field terms. Truth be told, I wanted to bail. I leaned over and whispered in Alex's ear, "This is the worst movie I ever saw!" Two thumbs down.

## Abort the Mission

A week after the orientation, I had appointments to meet two oncologists. Alex and I were en route to RUH, but this time a different building. I trudged up to the unfamiliar front desk and took a seat in the waiting room. The first thing I noticed was a lady coming out of a room, holding cotton batten on the inside of her arm. Jeepers! I clenched my jaw. After sitting for an undetermined length of time, my nerves frazzled. I was bouncing in my seat.

I finally went up to the front desk and blatantly asked, "Where do I go for blood work?"

The woman clicked away on the computer. "It doesn't show anywhere here that you need blood work. Let me just phone the lab to confirm." She talked for a minute, then hung up the receiver and delivered the best news I heard all year: "No, you don't have to."

"Yes!" I belted out, both my arms raised. This was so out of character for me because I usually didn't show a lot of excitement—except maybe if I won something.

From there, we waited for Dr. Kimosabe. He examined me and everything was copacetic. He was also the bearer of more good news: he didn't think chemo was the answer for me, so he kyboshed the whole idea. I sighed audibly.

The lady at the orientation had said that if anyone should need radiation, it was a fast procedure. "It will take you longer to find a parking spot," she joked. I didn't find this to be particularly humorous, as it wasn't about how long the treatment took; it was the fact that the procedure was harmful to the body.

As we waited now, the ward was like a monastery. The silence was killing me. I knew my mood depended on the words of the other oncologist.

Around the corner, I noticed a snack cart. This brought a smile to my face. The girl at the cart poured us coffee out of a thermos, then handed us our Styrofoam cups of "perk me up." She smiled with a toothy grin and asked in a chipper voice, "Would you like some cookies?" She held out the treats wrapped in plastic.

*Does a bear live in the woods?* "Would I *ever*!" My eyes lit up like a Christmas tree. I dunked the cookies in the coffee. I was content.

We moseyed on over to Ward A, where we met Dr. Brainiac. He confirmed that I had an astrocytoma + oligodrenglioma = oligoastrocytoma.

*Who in the what now? Easy for him to say*, I thought.

His sentence started out with, "I could write it down for you—"

"But you'd run out of ink," I interrupted.

He checked me over and came up with an answer I was all for: no radiation treatment. He explained the risks, that the treatment could affect my cognitive thinking, and believe you me, I didn't want to mess with my mental processing. I didn't want to tamper with the good brain cells, and heaven forbid, risk memory impairment. I agreed with him and figured we should leave well enough alone. I wasn't about to risk not remembering things, having difficulty solving problems, having slow reflexes, or not being able to make decisions.

After beating my brains out over whether I should go ahead with the treatments, it was all for nothing. I had a notion that I should prepare myself for disappointment, but who knew a person could ever have a good day at the Cancer Centre?

Angela Freriks

## A Wink and a Gun

It had been six weeks and I meandered into the hospital waiting room for another encounter with Dr. Flawless. I was expecting a mundane visit with nothing new to report… I was aghast when my eyeballs scoped out the same two police officers who had been there on my birthday the previous year. Sure as heck, I saw a prisoner rocking back and forth in his chair. He sat behind the wall with the door open; every now and then, I saw his bright orange toque bobbing in and out. I couldn't confirm that this was the same bad apple I saw before. I nudged Alex with my elbow and nodded my head towards him.

"Does he have chains on?" Alex muttered, doing his best not to look.

"Either that or he's got some animal in there with him," I whispered.

This was the first time we had spoken with Dr. Flawless since his skillful hands had performed the complex surgery. I spoke with body language: *Hey, you're the man!* I felt like winking and making the hand gesture of a gun, but then remembered the two cops standing out in the waiting room. Dr. Flawless would probably have failed to see the humour in me using my tongue, clicking like a cap gun. He and his colleagues, those surgeons with their staple guns, were sure to be a tough crowd.

I presented him with several questions. He fired his answers back. The man was sharp as a tack. He told me I could go back to normal, but the problem still remained. I didn't have a license, which *drove* me up the wall.

I wanted to get clean, so to speak, and get off the medication. I wanted to get that junk out of my system. Amongst my research, I'd found out this medication didn't respond to seizures when diagnosed with an oligoastrocytoma.

Two days ago, I'd thought I was done with all the hospital kerfuffle. It had been determined that I'd get an MRI in six months. Dr. Flawless had strict rules when it came to driving, if a patient had seizures. He affirmed that if I was willing to go for an EEG and all went well, he would wean me off the medication.

*Whatever it takes to get rid of the cotton mouth.* I agreed without any argument: "You betcha."

I asked him what the tumour looked like, wanting him to determine the substance I'd been carrying around in my cranium. He claimed it was hard to explain, but described the viscosity to be thicker than custard. My face must have looked like I was in excruciating pain because I wore a "sorry I asked" expression.

"The cells were growing where they weren't supposed to," Dr. Flawless, the most brilliant man I'd ever known, said. "It was quite difficult to get at. Even though I used a microscope, the swelling of the brain can conjure with the tumour, thereby making it hard to determine the difference. The tumour was right in the middle of your left and right hemispheres; I had to get underneath this surface area to remove the piece that joins the lobes together in the fold."

I didn't understand the physics of the whole thing, but from what I gathered there were flecks of diseased cells around the remaining tumour. These fragments (figments) of my imagination were scattered hither, thither, and yon. The abnormal cells were going to be monitored—almost like having a parole officer. They had better be on their best behaviour or they were going to get punished, with chemo or radiation.

## I'm at a Loss

It had been three weeks and I was running out of patience. I gave Dr. Flawless' secretary a call and asked if she had any inkling when my EEG exam would be scheduled.

"I was just curious if I would be receiving a call or a letter, or..."

She was short and to the point. "It looks like Dr. Flawless faxed a letter to the department on January 25. I have no idea how long of a wait that will be. It's not my department."

Grrr, I so disliked that saying.

"Here's a number you can call," the secretary barked. *Click.*

*Oh, you did not just hang up on me, you dirty rat.*

Rather than sit around drinking coffee and commiserating, I picked up the cordless phone and got a hold of the EEG Department. "Do you have any idea how long of a wait it'll be until I get my EEG exam?" I asked in an out-of-breath tone while pacing the floor.

"Our waiting list is beyond ridiculous." The woman on the phone inserted a laugh where laughter wasn't due. "It'll be about a year."

"A year!" I yelled. I'm sure she had to hold the receiver away from her ear.

There was no way I was waiting a year for this friggin' exam just to get my head wrapped up like the end of a hockey stick. I wasn't about to sit around and twiddle my thumbs. Why was the waiting list so long to get one's head spackled? The last time I'd had this test done, the woman had pasted so much goop in my hair that I looked like a grease monkey twisting wrenches. I was livid. I had to devise a new plan.

I speed-dialled Alex. "Since when is this electro whatchamacallit such a hot commodity?" he asked. "And why is there such a long waiting period?"

I was so upset that I choked on my words. I couldn't help but wonder when I could put this thing behind me.

## Going Forward in Reverse

I needed to move forward, but instead I seemed to be pedalling backwards. I had gone to all the trouble and fret of getting the gross glob of a glioma out, and yet I still wasn't able to live life to the fullest. I felt frustrated. My life was still restricted, along with my license.

I took the initiative of calling my license issuer. Her tone was cheery and she gave me a toll-free number to contact SGI. Without further ado, I did as she instructed. The switchboard put me through to commercial medical. I was tickled pink to find out that I could get my family doctor to let them know I was medically fit to drive after being seizure-free for three months.

When I got off the phone, I did a little jig and rubbed my hands together vigorously. I felt the presence of hope in the air. I grinned like a Cheshire cat.

### Are You For Real?
*February 15, 2012*

The day before had been Valentine's Day and love was in the air. But the next day, *bang!* Death wanted my business. I was sitting at my desk when I got a phone call from a funeral home, asking if I was interested in prearranged funeral planning.

"Nope, not interested," I said, catching her off-guard. "Your business might go under before me. Besides, I'm just sitting here recovering from brain surgery… and I don't want to think about being buried six feet below the land of the living."

The line went *dead*, in a manner of speaking. The stunned lady was as unresponsive as a vegetarian in a meat market. After buying some vowels and saying she'd like to solve the puzzle, she said, "I wish you all the best."

At least I gave her something to talk about that night at the dinner table.

### Bucket List

As they say, life happens when you're busy making other plans. After the disturbing call from the funeral parlour, Alex and I were reminded that we'd never been to Hawaii. Before the cranium conundrum, we had planned on jetting off on a tropical getaway. I even went so far as to withdraw U.S. cash; I clipped out articles and made an itinerary.

Unfortunately, there had been a change of plans, *mahola* very much. Instead, I made a snap decision to give the old tumour the heave-ho. As irony would have it, the vile and disgusting villain packed up and headed off for a vacation in California; he departed and I was still homebound, stuck walking the pavement.

All I could do was slather on the Hawaiian Tropic suntan lotion and sit in front of the kitchen garden doors with the sun beaming in. I put on some shorts, tank top, and flip-flops. I even put on a pair of shades and read a book. The south-facing sun was so hot in the kitchen that I burned my legs on the leather chair. I enjoyed my "staycation" with two faux palm trees bracketing me.

Our next sun destination will be spent admiring the exotic paradise of Hawaii. Our next climb will be the Diamond Head in Waikiki. My favourite nut is the macadamia, so I'd love to treat myself to chocolate-covered macadamia nuts and enjoy them with a hot cup of coconut macadamia herbal tea. Until then, hang loose!

## A Clean Bill of Health

Open up and say Ahhh...men. Although God chose not to heal me *completely*, and I did have to undergo brain surgery, I believe God is omnipresent. He was in the operating room, along with the surgical team, guiding the surgeon's hand. I am forever grateful to Dr. Flawless and his medical team. I've had no further neurological problems.

Two weeks ago, I wasn't in a position to dicker with Frikker. I told him I needed my license back—not today, but yesterday—and he told me it was too soon. Under my breath, I grumbled something along the lines of, "Always by the book, these people. Can't cut me any slack."

Two weeks later, I was slip-sliding back to Dr. Frikker's office. Snow had been falling from the sky all day long, but I was fully prepared to go out in a blizzard if I had to. Nothing was going to stand in my way.

## Cranium Crisis

"Fi–nal–ly," I said, enunciating every syllable. Dr. Frikker had a letter confirming that I was medically fit to drive and he'd faxed the incredible news to the license issuer. But I still had to play the waiting game, until I got the "green light" from the motor license issuer.

I was gearing up and raring to go! I hoped not to jinx it by putting the cart before the horse, but I did so anyway. Alex and I went tire shopping. "It'll be so nice to have new Gummy Bears on my car!" I said, enthusiastically.

I simply couldn't wait to send someone a text saying "OMW" (on my way), then lay a blackie, squawking my tires on the pavement as I tore down the driveway.

Lo and behold, I got my license back—and not a moment too soon. I'd gone practically five months without a license, and I was closing in on forty. Truthfully, I was just as happy the second time around as when I turned sixteen. One might say I was ecstatic—a word I had just introduced into my vocabulary.

My face lit up like the Fourth of July when I received the "you're good to go" letter in the mail. My feet barely touched the ground. I couldn't get to the insurance dealer fast enough. I got there just under the wire, as they were about to close for the day. I knew today was my last trek through the snow dealing with itchy thermal underwear.

I walked in, pulling my hoodie down, revealing my beaming eyes and exuberant perma-grin. The lady informed me that I needed to get a new photo taken, passport-style. After suffering through almost two years of wearing an unimpressed face, *now* she told me I needn't smile for the photo. *Pfft.* Yeah, right. I gave the camera my best criminal face, but on the inside my chains were broken and I was free—how could I possibly keep a straight face? My mug shot expressed a serious poker face.

*Es perfecto.* That night, I stood back, hands on hips, and looked in the mirror, waving goodbye to the collection of futilities that had cluttered my mind. I was totally at peace with the reflection I saw and knew that I now had a clutter-free space. The tumour that once had barged in and encompassed my brain no longer had a place there.

## The Grand Finale

My word! It seemed to take forever for my Grade Twelve graduation to arrive. I thought school would never end. In the same way, I thought this book would never end, but the story's over now. I hope you've enjoyed my company.

Without the trials and tribulations of the tumour trauma, no words would have found their way onto these pages. I've had a numb brain twice in my life: once, obviously, for the craniotomy, and secondly, from all the brainstorming needed to complete this book. When I titled the first part of the book "Let's Take It from the Top," (quite literally), little did I know the phrase would pertain to a brain surgeon's words before performing the procedure. It was pretty intimidating talking to my neurosurgeon. I tried to thank Dr. Flawless for his strategic job. I tried to think of something intelligent to say, but all I could come up with was: "Thanks for fixin' my head, there."

I'm happy to report that I no longer take any prescription drugs. Speaking of medication, now it feels like I'm on happy pills, with symptoms that cause me to be high on life! It's a combo effect of positive thinking, energy, and adrenaline… all having a feel-good response. I'd describe it as the feeling of being hopped up on sugar. That reminds me: I'm due for my caffeine fix. My brain is screaming for a freshly brewed cup of joe. I'm off to get me a piping hot java—and I'm doing drive-thru, because I can. *Vroom!*

## Epilogue

As a child, I remember hearing, "God is the same yesterday, today, and forever." If healing happened back in the Bible days, could it happen today, and could it happen to me? Could this be God's plan for me?

The miraculous, immediate disappearance of the tumour was my initial prayer. When it became apparent that surgery would be needed, my second request was to be able to find a neurosurgeon willing and able to perform the surgery. I needed someone I felt confident in. I'd been on an emotional roller coaster for almost two years, waiting for a solution. To my amazement, I found that neurosurgeon right in Saskatoon. This was an answer to prayer!

Reaching out for emotional and spiritual help gave me God's comfort and assurance that all would go well. Lots of people prayed for me, and that was reassuring. My surgery went smoothly and the seizures stopped immediately after the tumour was removed. The recovery period was faster than anyone could have anticipated. For me, my first breath after surgery was a miracle in itself.

In this age of instant everything—instant food, instant service, instant gratification, and instant answers—I hadn't learned to wait on

God. I hadn't put my complete trust in Him. I still had many lessons to learn.

I now believe that going through difficult times strengthens one's character and makes one more empathetic towards others. I'm more appreciative of the simple things in life. I now have a greater appreciation for my health, my family, for everything! I feel that I'm spiritually, physically, emotionally, mentally, and medically fit for whatever life has in store for me in the future. As they say: Shape up or ship out! Use it or lose it!

Every hour of every day is a new miracle. So, my words of wisdom are these: never take life for granted and cherish every moment. For those of you who have been blessed with good health, enjoy every minute of it!

I'm ashamed to admit that I was jealous of people with vibrant personalities during this trying time of my life. It was really hard for me to be around someone with great exuberance when I could barely crack a smile some days. We all know or have met people who are jovial all the time. Maybe you *are* that person. These people act like they're king of the world. They act like they're invincible or indestructible, that nothing bad will ever happen to them. They may have a perfect bill of health, be wealthy, or have a high education, with letters behind their name. Maybe they've never lost a loved one. Their lives are hunky-dory, so to speak.

My personality type is far from enthusiastic. My husband jokes that even if I won the lottery, I wouldn't jump and down about it. All I'd say, in a monotone voice, is, "Sweet."

I'm thankful, today, for the change I've seen in my life. This life-altering situation has resulted in a change of attitude. I give all the credit to God. I live each day and try to make the best of my situation. Through my experience, I hope to empower others. God gives us free will. We have to make our own choices. I want to encourage you to make the right decisions in your life. Glorify God; it's through Him that I had the strength to get through this.

This experience has been a real eye-opener for me. It's up to you how to live your life. I needed a rude awakening to get my priorities straight. Material things don't mean as much to me today. I don't focus my life around working my fingers to the bone.

There's a worship song called *More Precious than Silver*. The lyrics tell us to focus on storing our treasures in heaven, not here on earth where dust, rust, and mould wither all things. As a wise man once said, "I've never seen a U-haul on the back of a hearse." You can't take your earthy possessions with you when you die. In the end, they won't mean squat. No matter how rich or famous you may be in this life, it too shall pass.

## Inspirations and Acknowledgements

First and foremost, I'd like to thank my parents for their never-ending support. I can always count on them, no matter what. Even though I was almost forty, when life threw me a curve ball, my parents rushed to my rescue. Mom and Dad have always been there for me before, during, and after my cranium crisis. Thanks, Mom—my corrections officer—for helping me polish up my grammatical errors.

To my husband of three years: little did you know you were saying "I do" to a woman with a brain tumour. Thanks, honey, for snapping me up; there's not too many of us "good ones" left. Thanks for putting up with me and my moments. Thank you for being my motivation to climb a mountain! I'll be forever grateful to you for being my best friend and chauffeur. My sincerest gratitude for driving me to all my appointments, visiting me in the hospital, and driving me everywhere but crazy. You're a hard-working man. I'm so glad I found myself a Mr. Fix-it around the house, yard, and vehicles… all but my head, and I know you would've fixed it if you could. You're one in a million.

To my mother-in-law: you're a *Super Mom* for raising two peas in a pod. After your little guy was born, a twin girl arrived as well. I appreciate you being there for me. Your prayers get answered and your faith shines through you!

To Laurie, Michael, and Clare: thanks so much for the prayers, encouragement, positive thinking, care package, and long conversations on the phone.

To my friends and family: thanks for thinking of me and showering me with phone calls, emails, texts, visits, cards, and gifts. Special thanks to those who came to break me out of house arrest. Thank you to my aunt Jannette, who said when giving me positive feedback, "I laughed, I cried, and proclaimed it was a great honour to be the first to read the first draft of the manuscript." Thanks to everyone for all the prayers and pledges towards our mountain mission. Special thanks to my uncle Virgil and aunt Halley for the prayers and hospitality (spoiling us with fresh homemade bread) while we were in Vancouver. We had a blast!

To the brain tumour support group: I hope I can help you overcome your fears, even though it's beyond a scary situation to deal with. I attend these meetings to share my feelings and my story with other like-minded people.

Special mentions: Gary and Karen, who put endless hours into the support group. Your time and energy is much appreciated. The thoughtfulness of you bringing over one single rose had such an impact. I gave Karen a draft copy of the first twenty pages of this book. When she told me she thought it was fantastic, I felt encouraged to press on and do the best I could to write more.

To Dr. Flawless: I sure wish I could give credit where credit is due, but unfortunately, I didn't feel I had the right to use your real name.

To FREE 100.3 FM, Saskatoon's Christian radio station: I listen to your music faithfully. I love all the uplifting songs. I play it at home, work, and in the car. I requested it in the MRI, but it wasn't music to my ears when they said no. (We should get a petition going, don't you think?)